Critical Mass

I never thought it would be like this...

by

Kathy Beckwith

Library of Congress Control Number 2003103188

ISBN 1-930572-25-5

Printing (Last Digit)

10   9   8   7   6   5   4   3   2   1

Publisher—
Educational Media Corporation®
PO Box 21311
Minneapolis, MN 55421-0311
(763) 781-0088

http://www.**educationalmedia**.com

Production editor—
Don L. Sorenson, Ph.D.

Graphic design—
Earl R. Sorenson

Cover art—
Greg Turner
Ken Karl

for two especially
and for many

with thanks to
Jesse Watson
John Lynch
Sharon Michaud and Gretchen Olson
and the teens and adults
who read the manuscript,
encouraged me,
and believed
that in telling the story,
understanding and good
will come.

Kathy Beckwith

Kathy Beckwith

Part I. ABE

My cousin Josh has this disease called Bell's Palsy. He got a headache one day, and his face hurt. The next morning when he brushed his teeth, he drooled toothpaste and spit down his chin.

The doctor told him to raise his eyebrows. Only one went up. The whole other side of his face wouldn't move. When he's serious, you don't notice it a lot, but when he smiles, it's like he has two faces, and you're not sure which one to look at.

My mom acts like it's some tragedy, like Josh's life is over if his face doesn't get back to normal. I wish she could understand that he's not so bad off. The doctors say a lot of kids get better. But even if he doesn't, he'll still be Josh.

I was thinking that I should trade faces with him some day, and maybe they'd finally figure out that something's wrong with me. It's not only on the outside that people can have two different faces.

Or maybe it's better if they never know.

1

Abe had almost reached the edge of the woods when he heard the siren. He hadn't planned an escape, but he felt he'd be safe if he could get across the open field into the trees. The siren grew louder, maybe another cop car on the way, or an ambulance. He wished the sound would stop so he could run. He couldn't run with a siren blaring in his ears. The smoke alarm shrilled on through his dream, bringing Abe back from the edge of the woods to his bed. His heart pounded. He opened his eyes and checked the time—6:27 a.m.

That meant the toaster or Maggie's shower had set the smoke detector off again, and not a fire. He rolled over and pulled the pillow against his ears.

"Can somebody yank that dumb alarm off the wall? I have three more minutes!"

"So just to get three more minutes of sleep, you're willing to burn alive in your bed?" It was Maggie, banging on his door. "We gotta get out of the house, Abe!"

Abe yanked the pillow off his head and flung it at the door. It slid silently to the floor as Maggie's pounding continued.

"Come on, Abe!"

"Get lost, Maggie!"

"Abe, you've got to get up. It's no joke," Maggie persisted.

"Dad, is that your toast?" Abe called out.

"Dad just left for work," Maggie answered.

"Mom!"

There was no reply. Abe rolled out of bed, kicked his pillow out of the way, and yanked the door open. A wisp of black smoke floated into the hallway from the kitchen. Maggie stood there in her worn out nightshirt, staring him in the face.

"We gotta go, Abe. Fire drill," she said over the blare of the smoke detector. "No joke." But she didn't move.

"Maggie, you are insane! Get out of my doorway!" Abe shoved her aside, grabbed his pillow, and swung it up in front of the alarm to clear the air. The screech stopped just as the music from his clock radio clicked on. 6:30. Abe threw his pillow at the radio, then swung the door closed behind him, calling back to Maggie, "...and you're indecent too!" His open palm hit the snooze button as he fell back onto the bed.

"Nobody is going to start my day that way," he said to the Einstein poster on his wall.

Half an hour later Abe awakened to the sound of Maggie's piano practice mixed with the music from his clock radio.

"Cutting it a bit close, aren't you, Abe?" his mom said as he walked into the kitchen. "I thought you were getting up early to finish your homework."

"Mom, when are you going to tell Maggie to quit playing fire marshal? I'm sick of her telling me to get out of the house for some fake fire drill."

"She's just trying to get us back to the plan, Abe. Fire drills aren't a bad idea."

"It was the middle of the night, Mom!"

"6:30 is not exactly the middle of the night."

"Well, it's insane to have a fire drill every time the smoke alarm goes off. With our toaster and the steam from Maggie's shower, we could be doing fire drills every other day."

"I'll remind her to turn on the exhaust fan."

"I thought we were going to get a new toaster," Abe continued.

"Been too busy. I'll try to buy one this week."

"She acts like she's in charge of my life."

"Buy a what, Mom?" Maggie asked as she bounded into the kitchen. Without waiting for an answer, she turned to Abe. "Who's in charge of your life?"

"Me," he said flatly.

Maggie had interrupted them. Abe had also wanted to ask his mom why she let Maggie run around the house in that old nightshirt. Not that he ever would, but it seemed like somebody besides him needed to do something about it. The other morning when the steam from Maggie's shower set the alarm off, Abe had jumped out of bed to yank it off the wall himself. But there was Maggie, standing on a kitchen chair, struggling to get the alarm down with one hand, clutching her towel with the other.

"Maggie, open it up and rip the battery out, or wave your towel at it, or something," Abe had yelled.

"Sure, and stand here naked?!"

"You might as well be," Abe answered her. Maggie didn't seem to realize how the towel draped when she climbed on the chair.

Kathy Beckwith

"Sorry. Sorry, Abe," Maggie yelled over the squeal of the alarm. "I'll remember to turn on the fan next time." Then she added, "Why don't you just get up at 6 o'clock like everybody else, and then we wouldn't have this problem?"

"What time I get out of bed is not the problem, Maggie," he had said as he slammed his door closed. But he hadn't explained further. It was easier to talk about fire marshals and toasters.

Maggie interrupted his thoughts. "What are you going to buy, Mom?" she repeated.

"A new toaster."

"Cool." Maggie turned to Abe. "Sorry about this morning, Abe. I would have let you sleep. But if you get used to sleeping through a fire alarm, and then some day there really is a fire, you might just stay in bed and burn up because you think it's the toast burning."

"Eat worms, Maggie."

"I already had breakfast, thanks."

"Abe, that's no way to talk to Maggie," Mom said.

Abe put a couple of pieces of bread in the toaster and stood over it to make sure they didn't burn. "I'm tired of her bugging me all the time."

"Golly, Abe. All I did was try to save your life."

"You're not 9-1-1, Maggie. I don't need you to save my life."

"That's enough," their mom said. "You guys better get ready for the bus."

"Can I take your car today, Mom?" Abe asked. "I'll never get my homework done by bus time."

"I need it."

"I'm going to start riding my bike to school," Maggie said, "when it stops raining. It'll save me twenty minutes over the bus ride. Want to ride with me, Abe, when basketball's over?"

"Hang on, Maggie," her mom said firmly. "I never said yes to that idea."

"Mom," Maggie pleaded. "I've been riding bikes since I was a baby. And I already asked Gabi to ride too, so you won't have to worry about me getting attacked in Rape's Gulch."

"It's Rabe's Gulch, Maggie. And that's not the issue."

Abe knew it was. He had overheard his mom telling his dad how dangerous the gulch was. Everybody knew the story about the girl from Mom's class who got raped there. A hundred years ago, in the middle of the night, when she was hitchhiking alone, drunk. Not exactly the same as riding bikes to school with a friend, Maggie had pointed out. But a lot of people remembered it, and that strip of road was called Rape's Gulch as often as Rabe's Gulch. It made no sense, but Mom had refused to let Maggie ride that way to town, even though it was the shortcut.

"Come on, Abe," Maggie said. "Bus time."

He smeared jam on his toast and headed for the door. He'd do his homework on the bus.

"See you after basketball, Mom," Abe called over his shoulder.

As they waited for the bus, Abe turned to Maggie. "How can dreams go for an hour and then end up with

Kathy Beckwith

something in your dream that fits perfectly, happening at the exact time it happens in real life? Like a siren going off or something."

"It doesn't, Abe. That's impossible. Your dream would have no way of knowing what's going to happen in the future."

"Maggie! Just listen to me for once."

"I did. And I told you the answer."

2

The bus unloaded in front of Mayfield High School. Maggie spotted her friend, Gabriela, heading for the science wing and the freshmen lockers. Abe wondered where Maggie got her Maggie-ness, like it didn't matter if half the school heard her yell, "Gabi, wait up!" That was Maggie.

Gabi whirled around and waved. "Go, girl!" she called back across the crowd. Abe stood where he was, watching as they met up, dropped their bags, and flung their arms around each other as if they'd been separated for ten years instead of a weekend. They made life look easy.

As much as Maggie irritated Abe, he had to acknowledge her loyalty and general niceness to friends. Gabriela had been at their house every week since pre-school, and Abe had never once heard Maggie put her down. It just didn't seem to make sense to Maggie to bad mouth people. She yelled sometimes, and insisted, like when she made Gabi be her Siamese twin for Halloween one year even when Gabi said it would slow them down from getting a lot of candy trick-'r-treating. Abe had agreed with Gabi, at which point she sided with Maggie and off they went around their neighborhood in one giant pair of bib overalls. Abe supposed that's why they had won the three-legged race at the end of school for the past six years in a row.

Kathy Beckwith

The sound of the next bus arriving behind him brought Abe back to the moment. He waited for it to pull up and stop. Eis and Trish were sitting together near the back. Abe could see that some big commotion was happening inside the bus. Eis piled his books on Trish and hopped back a couple of seats. He dropped out of sight for a minute, then came back up waving his lunch sack in the air. Everybody started filing out of the bus, laughing.

Eis talked to the driver as Trish bounded down the steps with her arms full of books, some lunch stuff balanced on top of the pile. She spotted Abe, smiled, and winked.

"Mouse," she said as she approached, as if that explained something.

Eis caught up with them almost instantly. "Don't drop my gingersnaps, Trish," he said as she slid his lunch and the pile of books into his arms. He turned to Abe. "Nobody else wanted to catch it. The driver went bonkers last night because some junior high dork let this mouse loose inside the bus. He threatened to turn around and take everybody back to school unless somebody confessed and caught the thing. We sat parked on the side of the road for a good five minutes. Nobody confessed, but the mouse disappeared so the driver finished the route. Then here it comes running around this morning just as we get to school. I didn't want to get stuck on the bus for another Inquisition, so I stepped on it."

"You stepped on a mouse?" Abe asked.

"Well, I would have, except these are my new shoes and I didn't want mouse guts all over them, so I caught it in my lunch sack instead." Eis stuffed his gingersnaps into his jeans pocket. "Hey, you guys won't mind carrying my bologna sandwiches in your pockets, will you?"

Abe sidestepped the outstretched bologna. Eis whirled behind him, unzipped the pouch on his backpack, and stuffed the sandwiches inside. "Hey, hold still, man. You're smearing mayonnaise all over your calculator."

"Eis! You nerd! Carry your own sandwiches."

But Eis zipped the pouch closed and kept talking. "That mouse acted like I was a headlight and he was a deer or something. It didn't even move."

They were at their lockers. Abe took the sandwiches out of his backpack and stuffed them on the shelf in Eis's locker. They headed for first period.

It wasn't a bad way to start the day, Trish's desk on one side of his, and Eis's on the other. Abe felt lucky to have them both. Eis had transferred in during their freshman year, and Abe was the student council rep the counselor chose to show Eis around the school. But it was actually Eis who took Abe around to parts of the school he'd never thought to look at—inside the janitor's workroom, up into the storage behind the stage.

"Hey, they told you to give me a tour, Lewis," Eis had said. "You'll never get rich doing tours of the halls and the johns. Do the underground, man. That's where the money is." Eis led the way to the back of the cafeteria where the cooks work and extended his hand to the first person they came to. "Hi! I'm Collin Eisenhower, but most folks call me *Eyes* for short," he said, "spelled E-i-s.

This is my first day here and I'm very pleased to meet you, Ma'am."

She shook his hand and asked if he was related to Ike Eisenhower. Eis answered, "No, but if it would get me one of those brownies to say yes, why then, I'm his favorite great-great grandson." The cook laughed and handed Eis a brownie. He shared it with Abe. Eis was like that from the very first day. Abe was glad when the tour was over and they hadn't gotten into trouble, but he was also glad he was chosen tour guide.

Abe had known Trish ever since grade school, and liked her that long too. Then last year when their youth group went up to Mt. Hood, he realized that Trish felt the same way about him. That was the first time she winked at him.

They would probably be going together officially if it hadn't been for Zach, their youth pastor. He had this three-point theory: Have a blast, be a friend, find God once a day. Abe didn't bother with the God part. He'd already tried that. It didn't work. It was easier to talk to Einstein. You didn't have to screen what you said. But Zach was good at planning blasts. He was the one who taught Abe how to skim board—how to throw the board and time the outgoing waves perfectly. He led the youth group and their flashlights through the old lava tubes south of Mount St. Helens. He organized the go-cart party. Abe liked him. He was fun.

So Abe didn't fight Zach too much on his friends theory, even though he thought it was over-kill. Zach got the kids to agree to group stuff, and to slow down on dating. He suggested not "going together" till they were seventeen, and only then if they thought they'd die if they didn't. He said it worked for him and Tess, his wife. He knew a lot of kids who were in complicated messes because they got involved too soon. Abe hadn't agreed to Zach's theory, but Trish had, so there he was. Sometimes Abe figured it was just a matter of words anyway, but other times he thought it would be nice to be able to use the words so everybody would know for sure that Trish was his.

Having Eis and Trish around made Abe feel normal, like what was going on in his head didn't matter so much.

3

"What do you think about the Quotation for the Day, Mr. Eisenhower?" Mr. R asked Eis as the first period bell stopped ringing. Abe glanced at the board and saw the quote:

"I hold it, that a little rebellion, now and then, is a good thing and as necessary in the political world as storms in the physical."
—Thomas Jefferson

Eis stood right up and said, "Mr. Rogers, last summer we had a hailstorm. I went outside and took my hat off and caught the hail and then I scooped it into my hand and ate it. In two minutes it was over. The stuff on the ground melted. But my stomach was cool all day."

"And the point of your discourse, Mr. Eisenhower?" which was Mr. R's way of asking if Eis was flapping his tongue or if he had anything to say.

Eis replied like it was totally obvious, "Rebellion does that, sir. Makes a person believe it could even snow in July. That things could be different than what everybody takes them for." Glancing again at the quote on the board to get a few key words, Eis continued, "Rebellion is something Thomas Jefferson, like me, would take his hat off for now and then."

"And I think he would find it a pleasure to discuss the matter with you, Mr. Eisenhower," Mr. R said. Abe figured that's probably why Eis stood up and didn't "pass" to somebody else, which Mr. R allowed. Because all day long Eis would be able to think of Thomas Jefferson asking his advice on revolutions and hailstorms.

The thing Abe really liked about Mr. R was that he made you feel like you were amazing. That your ideas mattered. But first of all that you even had ideas. Abe had a teacher his freshman year who assigned writing projects and then returned the papers with a check mark by the name to show she had read them. No grade. No comments. Just a check mark. That wasn't Mr. R. He must have run out of a hundred red markers a year. He wrote all over their papers, so it was always interesting to get them back and see what he said.

Abe knew a couple of kids who never turned in papers in other classes, but they did in Mr. R's. He figured it was because they liked the red marks talking back to them. Abe did. That and when Mr. R saw him after a basketball game and said "Great third quarter!"—the quarter he hit four lucky 3-pointers.

"Nobody's that lucky, guy. You're good at the sport," Mr. R added. He had even sat in on a couple of their practices, like he understood that it was the way they worked then that made the games happen. That the fire in your lungs and muscles and the sweat and the exhaustion were okay because you wanted to do it, for yourself and for the guys you had played with since junior high. It felt good to be noticed. Not just as Abe, but as a part of the team.

And Mr. R didn't throw out Abe's papers just because of the spelling. "You shall be victorious, Mr. Lewis," he had said. "It would be a shame to let talent go unrecognized because of vicious spelling." He had Abe memorize "Victor" and "Vic" and said he could give them both "i-o-u's" the next day.

"And now, to get us in the mood for Elizabethan poetry," Mr. R was saying to the class, I have invited my friend, Mr. Douglas, who also helps maintain our building, to step in and sing a duet with me. You may turn to page 157 in your texts, if you'd like to follow along." Abe couldn't believe it was an old Shakespeare poem. Mr. R and Scotty Douglas, the janitor, were really good. The kids whistled and started a chant for "Encore!" but Mr. R said he was still working on the music for the next one. It would be for a barbershop quartet, and did any of them want to join?

Then Mr. R had Jason, a kid in the class, do a rap of this 400-year-old poem called "Cherry-Ripe."

Abe described the rap to his mom when she came to pick him up after basketball practice that day. As always, he got halfway into the car and she said, "Hi, Abe. What great thing did you do today?"

"I started a sonnet, Mom. We all did. And Jason did this rap of an old time poem. It starts out 'There is a garden in her face.' Jason had to do that line three times because we laughed at him. But it goes on about this girl who won't kiss anybody till she's good and ready,

'Till Cherry-ripe themselves do cry.' 'Themselves' means her lips.

"Anyway, after Jason's rap, the girls started cheering and pounding on their desks, and the whole class laughed about Cherry-ripe, and it kind of made us feel that those old Shakespeare guys might have been regular people if they were alive today."

"I suspect so," she answered. "How do you think Shakespeare would like your English class, Abe?"

"I don't know. Pretty good. You know he got married when he was eighteen, Mom."

"Dumb," she responded.

"Most people don't call Shakespeare dumb."

"I just don't want you married in two years."

"Don't worry."

"What else?"

"What else what?"

"What else did you do today?"

"Talked about Critical Mass essays. But we have to finish *Macbeth* first."

They were pulling into their driveway when Abe asked, "Mom, don't you ever get bored asking me what great thing I did today?"

"No."

What he really wanted her to ask was, what trash thing did you do today? Just straight out like that. "Abe, you got any major garbage in your life?" she could say. Or "Anything we need to talk about, Abe? Anything bothering you?" But it was always, "What great thing did you do today?" like he was some hero kid who never thought about doing some things.

His mom was a lot like God, Abe thought. Always willing to listen if it's good stuff. But never asking about anything else, never suspecting there's something really wrong. Never noticing that he has mental Bell's Palsy.

4

Abe left the house the next morning, and then stuck his head back in the door. "Hey, Mom, I forgot to tell you, Trish invited our English group over to her place tonight to work on our video of *Macbeth*. You won't have to pick me up. Eis said he could get his dad's pickup and come get me after practice."

"What about dinner?"

"Mr. Carman is cooking some beans or something."

"Okay, see ya tonight."

Eis pulled up in front of the gym after practice got out. Abe threw his backpack in the pickup seat and hopped in. They were a couple of miles from Trish's when Eis rolled his tongue around on his teeth and said, "Hey, Abe, give me your toothpaste. My breath is rotten. Can't be kissing Sara with this mouth."

"Right! Wish on, man. There's no kissing scene in *Macbeth*."

"There is life after Macbeth, Lewis. I have offered Sara a ride home from Trish's and she has accepted. My mouth must be cool from the first moment she lays eyes on me. Tonight I may hear 'Cherry-Ripe'."

Abe laughed, but Eis went right on, "Ricardo said he'd give you a ride home. You don't mind do you?"

"No, that's okay."

"So give me the toothpaste."

"You gunna brush your teeth in here?"

"Come on, Abe. You always have toothpaste in your backpack."

"It's for my retainer. You're not using my toothbrush."

"I don't want your toothbrush, Lewis. Just the toothpaste. Hurry up, man. We're almost there."

Abe dug into the side pocket of his backpack and handed the tube to Eis. Eis had the cap off and a blob of toothpaste smeared into his mouth in seconds.

"Hey, don't swallow that stuff," Abe advised. "It rots your stomach."

"I don't. I spit it out."

With that, Eis rolled down his window, popped his head out, and spat.

"Gross! You're gunna have toothpaste spit all over the side of your...." He didn't finish the sentence. The angle of Eis' face hit the wind just right, and his glasses were hurtled from his face the same instant the spit left his mouth.

"Oh, crap! My mom's gunna kill me. Those are my new glasses."

Eis screeched to a stop on the side of the road, just within sight of the Carman's driveway. "Oh, man, how far back did those things land?" They both hopped out of the pickup and ran back down the highway, looking for the glasses, but saw no sign of them. Two cars and a farm truck came past.

The next vehicle to come along was Melanie's. "Need any help, guys?" she called out the window of her car. "Something blow out of the pickup?"

"Don't tell her," Eis said to Abe. "She'll tell Sara."

Eis turned away, so it was Abe who was left to answer. "No.... Uh, that's okay. We're looking for one of Eis's hubcaps. Tell Trish we'll be there in a few minutes."

"Okay. See ya then," Melanie called as she pulled back onto the road.

They resumed their search, Eis looking in the grass at the side of the roadway, and Abe a bit closer to the ditch.

"Don't you have some fancy prayer for finding glasses, Lewis?" Eis asked. "We're late to Trish's, I'm gunna be railed on at home, and besides I need my glasses to see. So pray, man."

"Come on, Eis. They're probably crushed to smithereens just from hitting the road, if they didn't get run over by that truck."

"Don't say that. I need 'em! Come on, Abe. You go to church. Say a prayer."

"Sure. Like prayers reassemble glasses or bring them out of the ditch. Okay, here's one for you:

'Good bread, good meat, good Lord, let's eat.'

"Hey," Abe continued, "you didn't close your eyes during my prayer. It probably won't work just because of that."

"Oh no? I see something!" Eis took off running down the road, much farther than the glasses could have been, it seemed to Abe. Eis stooped down, picked something up, and started waving his hand wildly in the air.

"Hey, Lewis! I found them!" He popped the glasses on his face and ran back towards Abe. "Let's go! We're late for the party." Eis hopped in and started the pickup. "What you doin', Abe? Let's go."

"Just checking your hubcaps, Eis. Can't lie to Melanie." Abe jumped in and turned to Eis. The glasses looked funny. The frame went too far up his eyebrow on one side, and one of the lenses was either dirty or scratched. But Abe didn't say anything. Eis took the glasses off, breathed on the dirty lens, rubbed it on his shirt, and seemed to think the crisis was over.

Trish met them at the door. "Find the hubcap, Eis?"

"Yup. They're all there!"

"And we're all here, waiting. So let's eat. Dad made a great dinner."

Abe liked Trish's family. She had a cool brother, Steve, in college in Seattle, her mom was an accountant, and her dad was a computer programmer. Mr. Carman taught their Sunday School class for two years when Trish and he were in fifth and sixth grades. Then he was transferred to some other town back east for a couple years, but the rest of the family stayed here. When he got transferred back, his old class threw a surprise party for him at church. Abe remembered that because Mr. Carman almost cried when he told Abe thanks. Abe figured if he ever ended up marrying Trish, he'd get a pretty good extra family.

"Soup's on!" Mrs. Carman called. The kids headed for the dining room. Abe was sure Mr. Carman had actually started a prayer, but maybe he was just clearing his throat to get ready to pray, when Eis piped up, "Hey, Mr. Carman! Let Abe pray. He knows this great one that would turn these beans here into T-bone steaks! It works miracles."

Abe threw Eis a "You jerk!" look. All he needed was to have Mr. Carman ask him to pray. But Trish said something about people are cutting back on red meat and her dad was proud of his chili recipe and Eis better be nice or he'd have to eat left-overs with Scoundrel, their dog. She laughed, and so did her dad, and then he said a regular prayer. Abe caught up with Eis in the family room and said, "Hey, you know that was no prayer. It was a joke thing Maggie brought back from camp one year. It had nothing to do with finding your glasses. You say one word about me praying, and I tell the whole toothpaste kiss story."

"Well, in that case, man, let's just get on with Mr. Macbeth."

5

"How'd your *Macbeth* video go last night, Abe?" his dad asked as he passed Abe the salad.

"Pretty good. Only we didn't get done. We had this big discussion about how it didn't seem very realistic without costumes."

"You should have asked me, Abe," Maggie chimed in. "I still have our old costume box."

"No thanks, Maggie. Mrs. Carman offered a couple of old capes from down in their basement. Trish got embarrassed when she came back with a big box of old Halloween costumes. It sort of stopped our work for a while.

"They had great stuff—Minnie and Mickey Mouse costumes that Mr. and Mrs. Carman wore, with black tights and long black tails hooked on, some monk robes, a pirate outfit, an old R2D2 mask from the original *Star Wars* and one of those plastic suits to go with it, and some more stuff. Then there was this princess dress Trish wore in third grade."

"I remember that!" Maggie said.

"Right, Maggie."

"No, I do."

"You couldn't have. You weren't even born then."

"Abe, I happen to be two years younger than you and Trish. And I do remember it. Me and Gabi and Trish were all getting babysat over at Carman's…. Remember that, Mom? We were doing a play of Rapunzel, who I said I wanted to be, with yellow crepe paper for my long hair. Only Trish ended up getting to be Rapunzel because she had a princess dress that was too big for me or Gabi. I was mad. It's light blue with ruffly net at the waist. I remember."

"You're insane, Maggie. Nobody remembers stuff like that. But you're right. It was blue.... Maybe Trish was the insane one. She got up and threw the dress in the trash. Said she always hated it."

"That's not true. She loved it," Maggie responded.

"That's what her mom said. She reminded Trish that it was her favorite dress-up. She started to get it out of the garbage, but Mr. Carman said to let it be. I guess Trish was mad we were spending more time joking over the costumes than working on our project. We decided just to do *Macbeth* like it was LA or some big city today, so we didn't really need costumes."

"So how do you do the witches stewing and brewing in Los Angeles?" Dad inquired.

"We didn't get as far as picking the witches. Wantta be in our video, Maggie?"

"Abe, be nice to Maggie," their mom interrupted.

"I am nice. Maggie would make a great witch, wouldn't you, Maggie?"

"I would if I wanted to, but that's not the point. The point is that you'll remember all the mean things you said to me when I'm dead, Abe, and you'll weep your eyes out."

"Sure, Maggie. I can feel the tears coming right now."

"Well, it's not so far fetched, you know. I found a lump in my breast the other day. It could have been cancer, you know."

"God, Maggie!" Abe said.

"Abe, we don't talk that way."

"Mom, tell Maggie how to talk. People talk about corn and please pass the salad at dinner. And here Maggie's blurting out what she's finding where. Do we have to talk about her chest? I'm done."

Abe got up and took his dishes to the dishwasher. He headed for the computer room, but then stopped and turned back toward the table. "So you don't have cancer do you?"

"No. Mom took me to Dr. Moore. She said it was normal."

Abe shook his head, feeling disgusted. "Maggie, you are insane." He walked into the computer room and pushed the door shut behind him. He sat down at the desk and stared at his math book. But he didn't open it. He sat there remembering how afraid he had been a couple of years ago when one of his nipples started to swell. He was sure he was dying of cancer, or he was turning into a girl, or something awful. He worried for two months before he finally went to the library and snuck around in the stacks to find some books on sex. He found one on growing up that said that often happens to boys as their hormones adjust and it normally just goes away. He had been nervous for another couple months, hoping nobody noticed, until he looked normal again. And here Maggie blurts it all out at the dinner table as if it's the evening news and it should be common knowledge, and she's already been to the doctor and found out she's fine.

Abe started to open his math book, then closed it and turned on the computer instead. He decided to get his Thoughts Journal paragraph done for the Critical Mass project before he started math. He opened a CRITMASS file and began typing:

"Abe Feb. 20 p.m. Thoughts Jurnal

Maybe I should right about my sister after all. Sometimes Maggie is the critical mass in my life. Insane mass, at least. Mass. No, ask Maggie. She calls it lumps. Lumps in brests. God, why do girls talk about their brests at dinner! I can say God on my computer, Mom, because I just decided I'm going to delete this whole page so don't git upset and now I can say anything I want.

"Mr. R do you like to read about brests? What else do you like to do with them? So how did Maggie find this lump, anyway? Run her fingers over her brests? And feel something that wasn't as smooth as the rest. Are your brests smooth now, Maggie? What about the nipples? How do they feel? God what's wrong with me? Maggie, git out of my head! Git away from me. Stop wearing that old nightshirt all the time. It's too tight. It shows your nipples, Maggie. Didn't you ever notice? Or is that what you want? And why do you have to talk about your brests in front of me?"

Abe moved the curser to the top of the page, then clicked Select All. But instead of hitting Delete, he glanced

Kathy Beckwith

over his shoulder at the door, then back at the screen, clicked the mouse, and started typing again.

"You said this was a thoughts jurnal, Mr. R. You'd be surprised at some of my thoughts. I am."

The words scared Abe. He'd been managing up till now. He'd feel crappy at night, stressed out, or maybe okay, but in either case, he could just junk it all and get a good feeling on before he fell asleep. He'd look up at the Einstein poster and say, "Hey, don't bug me. Everybody does this." And Einstein didn't bug him. Except sometimes when he pulled the magazines out from under the bed, or replayed some of the hot scenes from the movies he'd seen. Abe would have to remind Einstein that people said he was dorky too. Didn't even wear socks to important meetings. And it somehow made Abe feel that Einstein wouldn't worry, that his thoughts were safe with Einstein.

But this computer journal was different. And Abe knew what it was. Maggie was getting mixed up in his stuff now. The other night Abe had let his mind bring Maggie into a movie in place of a girl in a towel who had asked for a back rub. And then he let her roll over, like the girl in the movie, so he could do her front too. It felt good.

Seeing "Maggie's brests" written on the screen was freaky. What was frightening was that he wanted to see them. Not the words. Her breasts. For real. And this time he wanted to touch them. All over.

He felt sick. He hit Select All and Delete in quick order. He didn't exit his file right then. He wanted to look at the blank screen. He opened his math book, but occasionally glanced back at the computer screen, relieved to see it was empty. Abe was glad to have his thoughts gone.

He noticed for the first time that he was sweating. He'd do his paragraph later. He had to get out of the house, go on a bike ride, or something.

Maggie was in the kitchen as he walked past with his bike helmet in his hand. He didn't look at her. Maggie was too good at reading faces.

"Isn't it too late for a bike ride, Abe?" she said. He didn't answer, but kept walking toward the door. "Hey, hold on then, and I'll go with you."

Abe couldn't think of what to say. Maggie had totally caught him off guard. She couldn't want to go with him. But Maggie just assumed his silence meant it was fine. She ran into her room for her helmet and joined Abe in the bike shed.

"Great idea, Abe. I was suffocating in the house too."

So Maggie could read minds. If she knew he was suffocating, did she know the rest? He glanced sideways to see if Maggie could see the garbage in his head. She was wheeling her bike out of the shed. When she glanced up, she smiled, hopped on her bike, and started for the driveway. Abe was right behind her.

"How about the Old Highway?" she asked.

"Okay with me," he said. They turned down the street that came out at the Grange Hall, then took another left onto the Old Highway. There wasn't much traffic there. The trees were big and hung out over the road, a good place to ride. After a few minutes Abe started to relax. He was glad they had come riding. It made life seem normal. Abe's thoughts were pushed aside when he realized they were approaching the hill.

For as long as Abe could remember, Maggie had tried to beat him up this hill. At first he crested the top when she was about halfway up and had to stop and push her bike. Then when she got a mountain bike for her birthday, she could pedal the whole way, but Abe still always beat her. The challenge had almost become a ritual. When they got to the Lost Valley Road turn off, Maggie would call out, "Wantta race, Abe?" "Sure, if you don't mind losing," he'd call back. And they'd be off. The first few times Abe had sailed down the other side and then had to sit and wait for Maggie, wondering if she'd been hit by a car or something. So he just got in the habit of waiting for her at the top of the hill. She'd come up huffing and puffing and say, "But I'm getting better, aren't I, Abe?" He never really wanted to hurt her feelings, so he always said, "Maggie, someday you'll come in a very close second." And off they'd go, over the top, sailing down the hill with the wind whipping against their faces.

Abe instinctively sped up when he saw the Lost Valley Road sign. Maggie did too and yelled out, "Wantta race, Abe?"

"Sure if you don't mind losing."

Abe pumped harder than ever. It was as if he were pouring extra fury into the pedals. He got to the top of the hill and glanced back. He was surprised to see that

Maggie was still pushing it and was just 10 or 15 yards behind him. "Hey, I'm getting better, aren't I, Abe?" The way she said it didn't really sound like a ritual anymore. It was as if she really believed she might beat him some day. He hardly had time to say "close second" when Maggie crested the hill and started down the other side. "Come on, Abe" she yelled over her shoulder.

They pulled up to the bike shed in the total dark. It had been too late for a bike ride, even with their lights. They left their helmets on the porch and walked in quietly so their folks wouldn't notice.

Abe sat down at the computer feeling good. He called up his CRITMASS Thoughts Journal and began typing where he had left off in his journal at school:

*"**One more thing about basketball:** People can git bogged down in all the stuff they do and forgit how much exercise can help you git rid of tension and crazy thoughts."*

He went back and deleted "crazy thoughts" and changed it to "stress."

"It feels good to work hard, it feels good to try to beet somebody, it feels good to be first, and even close second isn't to bad."

Abe almost added something about the wind whipping against your face, but then remembered he was talking about basketball. He looked back at what he had written. He was afraid it might not be enough, so he did a short paragraph on Maggie too, or rather on Insane Sisters. It wasn't next on his list, but the other things he had thought about would have taken too long. He ran the spell check, then reread what he wrote. It wasn't especially good, but he had math to do.

The light was still on in the family room when Abe went to bed, but the house was quiet. He glanced up at Einstein as he entered his room. "Good night," Abe said. He pulled his jeans off and lay down on his bed. He heard a clunk from Maggie's room, like she might have rolled over and knocked her elbow against the wall. He wondered if Maggie was asleep, in her night-shirt. He wondered what she was dreaming about.

Abe rolled over and slid a box of old t-shirts out from under his bed. He reached down into it, and pulled out one of the magazines buried at the bottom.

"Sure you want to do this?" he asked Einstein silently, but his hand didn't pause.

Abe reached up and turned off the light. He opened the magazine and spread it out on his bare thighs so that the yard light from outside the window shone directly on the pictures. He flipped through the pages. A pair of lacy lavender underpants marked the place he had used last night. He looked up at Einstein. "You gunna watch?" he asked the poster.

6

"You might want to take a minute to glance at yesterday's Thoughts Journals before we start in again today," Mr. R said to the class as he handed back Monday's journals. "Feel free to include in your new journal any response you might have to my commentary in red. I saw evidence of great minds at work, ladies and gentlemen, and I appreciate your efforts." He handed the papers back, and the room became silent as eyes scanned red marker.

I've been thinking a lot about the Critical Mass *super!*

Essay ever since we first talked about it. The idea

I think so too!

is good but I don't know if people can really write

about the thing that matters most to them. Some

Hmmm...

things are better if you just keep them inside, aren't

Potential

they? Maybe we should combine this class with

Environmental Science because we're already

doing a research paper in there on Old Growth

Forests & that's probably the most critical issue for

anybody to write about now anyway. If Mr. Thompson

approves, will you go for it, Mr. R?

I'll like to learn more.

Certainly, but could we
hold off on this a few
days & see what other
ideas you might want
to consider?

I hope many feel its
importance personally.
That is what I intended
for the Critical Mass
Essay. I want it to be
something that really
matters to you, Trish,
now.

M.R.

*I'll have to think on this.
Perhaps you are asking
yourself, though, & not me.
What do you think?
What kinds of things?*

*I hope they can.
What do you think
will prevent it?*

You'll be a Methuselah, Eis!

Humor can be a great tactic. I suspect we often take ourselves too seriously.

I hate to admit it, Mr.R, but right now I can't think of anything very critical. I always figger when something *Hmmm...* gets too critical that's the time to make a joke out of it. You live longer that way. Come to think of it I could write about those guys in Tibet (?) that live to be 13¢. Being healthy when your old is pretty critical. I think I read once why they think they live so long., but I forget now. Probably they're all vaudeville comedians and do shows in the mountains. Is vaudeville a place or a thing, Mr.R?

Yes! Essay potential? Young? people don't often mention this.

Where could you find that info?

I don't recall that being a major premise... but?

Hey, that reminds me. Somebody told me once that people in the Bible lived to be 7¢¢ or 9¢¢ or something. Is that a bunch of bull or what? And if it's true why doesn't somebody find out how they did it?

What do you say? Kings?

Methuselah again!

Hey, this is a BIG paragraph! How bout a little extra credit for old Eis?

...especially when you started out not able to think of anything! Bravo!!

My good man, 16 is a mere drop in the bucket compared to 130 or 969. Ask me again when you are old!!!

M.R.

Kathy Beckwith

Abe Lewis
Feb 18
(Class)

C.M. Essay--Possible Ideas

1. Basketball
2. Bike Trips to Mexico
3. Church Problems Required Church
4. Insain Sisters
5. War
6.

Evaluation

Basketball: This could be pretty interesting because it really is a big deal for a lot of kids, me included. I'm not sure if it's critical in the sense of critical mass, but it is a lot more importent than most things. The essay could have storys about how basketball really makes a diffance in people's lives a long time after they played it, how it keeps people in shape, how it's fun and makes people get along who normally wouldn't, etc. Scope. Definitely!

Bike Trips to Mexico:

to be continued. Times out.

Abe was still reading the notations in red as Mr. R explained that they'd do their journaling a little differently today. He wished that school could slow down sometimes. If this stuff was really critical, there should at least be time to think about it.

The timer caught Abe's attention, so he left his thoughts for the instructions Mr. R was giving.

"I'll set the timer for 12 minutes," he said. "Don't worry about finding the perfect word at this point. Just get some more ideas out on paper. Let one idea spark another."

He looked around at the class and concluded, "All right. Let's think Critical Mass, and then write until you hear the timer ring."

When the time was up, Mr. R said to pass their papers down the row, along with the journals they'd done for homework the night before. Trish grabbed up her pencil and scribbled over what she had written. "Put it under yours, Abe," she said as she handed it along.

The word "UBVRDY" jumped out at Abe. It was something misspelled, he knew. He didn't know the word, but he wondered if he'd be able to spot the right word on his spell check.

"What's ubvrdy, Trish?" he whispered. She seemed to flounder a bit, and then, as if she were irritated at him for asking, blurted out, "Some exotic African tribe, Abe. Just pass my paper on under yours."

"An African tribe? Come on, Trish," he joked.

Kathy Beckwith

"Abe. It is. Okay?!" Her answer was serious and final, and she sounded mad, so Abe let it go.

He was thinking about the incident when his mom pulled up to get him after basketball. He didn't even let her finish "What great thing did you do today?" when he asked, "Ever read anything about the Ubvrdys in the National Geographic, Mom?"

"Give me the general category, Abe—animal, people, or mountain range?"

"People. Trish says they're an African tribe."

"What country?"

"She didn't say. You don't remember them, huh?"

"No, I don't think so, but that wouldn't mean I hadn't seen something on them. They could have done the article ten years ago, and the name would have slipped me. Why don't you do a periodical guide check? Doesn't your library have that on computer?"

"Oh, it's not that big of a deal. I just wondered." He paused for a moment, just long enough for his mom to insert, "So, I didn't catch your answer, Abe. What great thing did you do today?"

"Well, actually I made a three pointer today in practice, way out from the left side. It was beautiful. I don't think I could ever do it again."

"You'll have to. I didn't see that one."

Abe glanced at his mom. She was totally serious. He would have to do it again, he thought, so she could see it.

7

On Wednesday Mr. R handed back another set of Thoughts Journals. Abe read the questions in red under his heading "Insane Sisters." It dawned on him that the reason nobody talks about something hard, is that you don't have to. There's no time. So if you ignore it, even a question, nobody notices. And time passes and they forget totally. Like Mr. R or anybody would do about the questions on this journal.

It was interesting that Mr. R had a sister too. Abe wondered if he ever looked at his sister's chest, when it was changing. Or maybe that's something that isn't supposed to be interesting. It seemed to Abe that guys can notice any other girl's boobs, but if they belong to your sister, you're supposed to pretend they're like a shoulder or a knee or something.

Something that doesn't belong in a Thoughts Journal.

Abe Lewis, home page

You make excellent use of your spell-check, Abe! I think you're winning!

Critical Mass Essay Possible Ideas, cont.

One more thing about basketball: people can

get bogged down in all the stuff they do

and forget how much exercise can help you

I need to remember this. Thanks.

get rid of tension and stress. It feels

good to work hard, it feels good to try to

beet somebody, it feels good to be first,

and even close second isn't to bad.

No, it isn't. Especially when you've worked hard.

Insane Sisters: I put this on the list

Yes. Negatives can challenge us too!

because you said to include positives and

negatives that we think about. It's not

I recall this from personal experience, but also the fun...

always fun having a sister. There are some

hard things that nobody talks about.

This last sentence leaves me curious, Abe.
—What are the hard issues?
—Why are they not talking about it?
Relationships are certainly one of life's critical
concerns. Do you want to explore this further?

M.R.

Monday, Feb 18

(Home)

This may be short since I really don't have much new to say since this morning. If I don't write about old people, maybe I'll do it on (why people fight). I can get a new case study every night. Come to think of it, I don't think they know why thy're fighting. So much for research!

I could also write about why people think school is so important when the native Americans never went to school & they managed fine--for a long time. I could also write why nobody thought I needed (a horse) & now it's too late. Or if I personally will ever die. How is that for critical mass ideas?

M.R.

Margin annotations:

This could make an evening somewhat difficult, no?

Now that I've read the entire page, Mr. Eisenhower I believe you have much new to say!

Many people would be interested.

Not necessarily. There are other resources. Perhaps you could ask the conflictees & see what they say.

What factors were at play here?

Did you?

What's your hunch, Eis?

Is it ever too late?

I'm quite interested in the variety.

You may be the one who could bring some powerful ideas into education, Mr. Eisenhower. How did the learning occur? How could that apply to young people today? Essay potential!

This may be a unique experience that many have not had. It could be the basis of a very interesting essay!

Feb. 18, home - Trish Carman

    Other ideas are the Holocaust and
Wow!
Therapy Dance. I saw a <u>demonstration on</u>

<u>that once</u> and it was really cool. (not the

Holocaust. I mean on how people in wheel-
Trish, this is fascinating info that I am not familiar with.
chairs and with m.s. could get better by

dancing) You said you mostly wanted us to

think about this and write our thoughts
Thank you for putting effort into this project
down as they come. I've been <u>thinking a</u>

<u>lot,</u> Mr. R. A lot! But my journal's in my

head. I'll give you an example: What's in

your head is safe. What is on paper can be
Is it?
seen. <u>Better to be safe than seen.</u> After

all, the world is <u>based on pretending so</u>

<u>that you can be normal.</u>

That's okay! Part of the project is to let you see what happens when your "head journal" begins to touch paper.

Is pretense normal, Ms. Carman? I don't know. I'm simply asking. You perhaps feel that it is. Can you pursue this thought?

I'll need to ponder this. Perhaps you can too.

ubvrdy!   *I don't know this word.*

ubvrdy = c.m. 4t.c.   *...nor this equation! Hints?*

M.R.

On Thursday of the next week, Mr. R handed back another set of Thoughts Journals and said his marker went dry. They could call a halt on their journals. He gave them the last half of the period to work in small groups to explain why they chose their essay topic. He wanted them to be sure they were committed to it.

Trish, Eis, Trevor, and Abe made a circle of their desks.

"Ladies and gentlemen, may I be the first to defend my thesis?" Eis asked. They smiled and nodded.

"The most critical mass in my life right now is that my folks are driving me crazy. They fight all the time. They need my shrink more than I do. The fact is, I can't stand to be around them, and I would much rather live by myself."

Abe couldn't help but smile. Not to make fun of Eis. He knew Eis was telling the truth. He'd been to their house. Eis's folks didn't even try to pretend when he was there. It was nothing to laugh about. He smiled because Eis was amazing. He could talk about anything. A bit like Maggie, he thought. And make it sound almost normal.

Abe remembered how he had felt the last time his own mom and dad had argued. They never did fight like swearing at each other, but they got mad at each other, and Abe hoped they didn't get a divorce over something as dumb as his dad thinking he could drink out of his mom's water bottle whenever he wanted. Because they kiss, he said, so what difference did it make, and since when is a little water really worth all the fuss. And she

Kathy Beckwith

was mad because he never bothered to bring one of his own and he could keep his mitts off her water, she didn't demand much for herself, and that was totally reasonable. Then there'd be this uncomfortable feeling in the air when they were around each other. They always seemed to be fine later on, but it was no fun while it was happening. Abe never told anyone how much it bothered him, not even Maggie.

And here was Eis, saying so casually that his folks need a shrink, and smooth as glass admitting he went to one, which Abe knew but always figured nobody else did, that Eis would keep it a secret, like he would if he ever had to go to a shrink. He had asked Eis once why he went, and Eis had stretched up tall and started waving his arms around in the air like he was some wild ape-man and said, "So as I don't tear you apart in a fit of fury, Abraham," and then he had just laughed and added, "Don't worry, man. I hardly ever get wild these days." Abe didn't worry. The worst Eis would ever do was make somebody die laughing.

"But I will go totally off my rocker if I try to research why step-dads treat their wives like dirt and why mothers do not do one blasted thing about it but yell, so in order to retain my sanity, I am writing about organ donations," Eis concluded.

"You donating some organ to a church, Eis," Trevor quipped.

"Hey, you know what I mean, man. Giving your eyes so some kid gets your cornea if you die but your eyes are still okay. Stuff like that. You kick the bucket, but not everything in your body is wrecked, so you give the good parts to somebody who needs it."

"I know what you mean," Trevor said. "I was just joking. I think I might want to be an organ donor too."

"So we're supposed to ask you why this is critical to you personally, Eis," Trish questioned.

"It's because of my Uncle Mike. The more I think about him dying, the madder I get. They bury people all the time who could have let Uncle Mike live if they would have just given him a liver.

"He took me out to his barn one time and said, 'Hey, Eis...' Well actually, he said 'Hey, Collin. It's high time you learned how to ride a horse.' Man, he knew I wanted to so bad, but my mom had said she'd bust my butt if I messed with any of Uncle Mike's horses. So he calls my mom on the telephone and talks to her for an hour about how safe I'll be, and then finally promises her he'll be right there with me. Just because she got dumped off when she was a kid and broke her arm.

"So anyway Uncle Mike calls into the shop and says he has a family emergency come up and he can't come in that afternoon. They think he's probably bad sick again, and what it is, is he rides horses with me all afternoon. And we went in and got some bread and peanut butter and then we rode again until dark. Man, I could hardly walk the next day, my butt and my legs were so sore. And then two months later he's dead because nobody gave him the liver he needed."

Eis was quiet. Finally Trish spoke up. "I think you'll do a good job on your topic, Eis." Abe and Trevor agreed.

Kathy Beckwith

"What about your African tribe, Trish?" Abe asked.

Eis drummed a bit on his desk and then said, "I relinquish the jungle to Ms. Carman."

"Let Trevor go first," Trish replied quietly.

"Okay, the jungle waits. Trevor, you're on," Eis said.

Trevor defended his choice of basketball as a topic, and what he said sounded to Abe better than anything he could come up with. Abe had narrowed his down to basketball and war, and as Trevor talked, he began to feel he'd better go for war. When Trevor finished, Eis asked, "Okay Abe, what hot topic did you decide on?"

The thought came to Abe that maybe he ought to tell the hot truth: The most critical mass in my life right now is Maggie's chest always getting in my way. And wondering if all girls sleep naked like the ones in my magazines. And that I've been lying to my folks about what kind of movies I see. Right. And then he'd drop dead.

"Well, I'm not exactly totally sure," Abe began. "But since we have to have our topic today I guess maybe I sorta might want to do it on war."

"We can tell this is a very critical topic to you Abe, maybe sorta, not totally exactly, but might be," Eis joked.

Abe knew he didn't sound very convincing. He wasn't sure himself he wanted to do it on war. But if basketball was out, then war was okay. It was a topic that had started to bug him. Mostly for that reason. That most of the people he knew considered it "a topic." Something to talk about. Not something real. Except that friend of his Grandpa Lewis's who hadn't gone to the beach for over fifty years because it reminded him of stuff that happened in World War II. Abe always figured he'd ask Grandpa Lewis if he could talk to the guy sometime, but then he decided the man would think he was weird or he wouldn't want to talk. Abe suddenly realized the kids were looking at him, waiting for his explanation.

"Well," he began. "I saw a couple of movies a few months ago..."

"Whew, Abe. You gunna tell the group about those movies?" Eis interrupted. "This should be a very interesting report, folks."

Abe could feel his face getting red. "They were war videos," he said. He ignored Trevor's laugh and continued quickly, "One was about these soldiers in World War II, or maybe World War I, who were regular people..."

Eis interrupted again, "What do you think soldiers are, monkeys or something? They're all regular people."

"No, I mean, they were kind of like me. Only maybe a few years older, but not much. They felt things. I mean they got scared when they thought the Germans were coming into their place. Their voices got all shaky. You could hear them breathing. Then they made friends with these German soldiers, well not right off, but after they realized they knew the same song, and they showed pictures of their families to each other. Anyway, in case you see it, I won't tell you the rest, which isn't cool, but that one and *Schindler's List* made me decide that somebody has got to start saying that war is totally insane."

Not like Maggie is totally insane, he thought. Really insane. He paused, but nobody said anything.

Abe began to feel more sure and continued, "For part of my research I'll look up some stuff on rules in war. I mean, I read in the newspaper once that countries agreed to what information you have to give if you're captured. Kind of like it's a game that has to have certain rules. But then they blow people up and somehow that's in the rules too.

"And we saw this Power Point program in youth group that some kids from Washington made..."

"I think about that too," Trish said, knowing the program Abe was talking about.

"They showed pictures of this cool city and the people doing all kind of things, little kids playing and stuff, and then it went black and it's just sounds of this debate going on about going to war. And when the pictures start again, they're the same pictures we saw before, only being destroyed—burned and blown up and torn apart, in with other war pictures. It ended with this group of kids we saw earlier who had been jump-roping in a building with a mural on the wall behind them, buried in pieces of the mural, the ropes tangled around, dead. It was so bad."

Abe stopped, not really being done, but not knowing what else to say. So Trevor asked the required question, "So why is this critical to you, Abe."

"Well, it just seems like it's something about the world that's whacko that people keep accepting as normal, and it's got to change."

"And you're going to figure it out, and then tell everybody, and then change the world. Right, Abe?" It was Eis, but it wasn't a putdown. He looked at Abe seriously, and added, "Yah, it is junk. I think you'll have a lot to write about."

"Good luck, Abe," Trevor laughed. "They've been having war for as long as there have been people. In the old days they dumped hot oil on their enemies from the castle walls and boiled them to death. Nowadays they just blow their heads off. War works. It's dumb to fight it." Then he realized what he had said. "Not dumb to fight a war. I mean dumb to try to change things."

"Hey, Trevor, don't underestimate my friend, Abe Lewis," Eis said. "This is a good man." Then he turned to Abe. "You may have to put a new twist on it, Abe. Like make it really humorous or something so people will pay attention."

"Make war humorous, Eis?" It was Trish. "That would be about as easy as writing a funny essay on donating your organs when you die."

"Good idea, Trish. I'll try it," Eis answered. And Abe had a feeling that Eis would find a way to make his essay funny. There was something funny in his brain. Abe remembered the time Eis did a What's-up-in-the-world" report on some big name clown from Poland who died. He had seen him on TV and said he was hilarious. Eis ended his report saying that he figured the clown's biggest regret in dying was that it was because of a stroke and not something really funny that would make people crack up when they were trying to be sad.

Abe remembered Mr. R smiling but saying, "Death is difficult to make light of, Mr. Eisenhower, even for a clown."

But Abe had thought it was totally logical for Eis to think that way. He made life funnier and better for Abe, so he probably thought being funny would probably make dying a little better too, since it happened to everybody sometime. Maybe. Abe caught himself wondering once or twice how somebody could die in a way that would make people crack up. He couldn't think of anything. He decided it was just as well. Dying should be sad. Even Eis had been pretty quiet when he told about his Uncle Mike.

"Okay, Trish. Your turn," Eis said. "Let's not keep the natives waiting any longer."

"Eis, 'natives' is a derogatory term, culturally biased," she replied.

"Who told you that, Trish? Why did we change Indians to Native Americans then? I thought that was cool."

"Forget it. I don't have anything to report on anyway."

"Hey, we gotta start research next week. Where'd you hear about this tribe anyway? What country are they from?" Eis pursued.

"Ubvrdy," Abe answered. He had liked the sound of the name and found it easy to remember.

"Hey man, I may be dumb in geography, but I know there's no country in Africa called Ubvrdy."

Trish came to her own rescue. "It's not a country. It's the name of the clan. They live in ..." She paused, then finished... "Uganda."

"Yah, that sounds cool, man. The U-ganda Ub-vrdy. But what's so critical? They becoming extinct or something and you don't want their good cannibal recipes lost from civilization?"

"Come on, Eis. You're being weird." Trish said.

"Okay. But why'd you choose them instead of the rain forest?" Eis took the voice of Mr. R: "The point of your discourse, Ms. Carman?" and added in his own voice, "Or are you just mouthing off?"

"I'll defend my own topic to myself, thanks." Trish jerked her desk out of the circle.

"Hey, Trish, no offense intended. I was being a smart mouth. Didn't mean to hurt your feelings or anything." Eis glanced at Abe, but Abe didn't know what was going on and simply shrugged back.

Eis continued, "Really, I'm curious about this African tribe. Tell us."

"It's nothing. I'm not even going to do my essay on that." The way she said it let them know it was the end of the conversation.

The bell rang and they gathered up their papers. As they passed Mr. R, Trish threw a note on his desk and said, "I'm finding a new topic." Abe tried not to look their way, but he did listen. Mr. R said something about it not being too late to switch topics, but he'd like to talk with Trish after school some time.

What's so touchy about the Ubvrdys, Abe wondered. He looked at Eis.

"Maybe she's having a bad day," Eis whispered. "If I hurt her feelings, I'll talk to her on the bus tonight."

Abe decided Trish didn't want their company anyway. He walked on ahead with Eis.

After lunch he went into the library and checked the encyclopedias. He got some help using the computerized periodical guide. Nothing anywhere. Maybe Trish was discouraged because there wasn't any information on the Ubvrdys.

8

Abe waited for Trish and Eis's bus Monday morning. He hadn't seen either one of them since Friday. Trish hadn't come to the game Friday night, or at least he couldn't find her afterwards, so he went on home with his folks and Maggie. Abe was anxious to see Trish now. He wasn't used to having her mad at him.

As the bus pulled up, Abe spotted her through the window and tried to see from her face what kind of mood she was in.

She stepped off the bus and gave him a big smile and a wink. Whatever had upset her Friday was obviously over.

But in first period when Mr. R gave them a few minutes to finish up their group work before class discussion, Eis announced that their group had finished.

"What about Trish?" Abe asked.

Eis shook his head, and the look in his eyes said, "Not now."

It bugged Abe a little. Eis was suddenly putting himself in charge of protecting Trish, and Abe didn't like the feeling it gave him. Besides, if there wasn't much information available on the Ubvrdys, Abe figured Trish had better face up to that now and change topics. He felt irritated at them both.

Abe realized that his thoughts had carried him away from the class. He hadn't heard the front row of kids tell

Kathy Beckwith

what they were working on. He wondered what he had just missed as Jenny's quickly crossed eyes and comment brought a roar of laughter from the class. Everybody had turned to look at Trish, and Trish was obviously back in her mood.

"I'm not doing a report on the Ubvrdy tribe," she said. "That was all a mistake. I'm looking for a new topic." Trish turned to Abe, and with anger in her voice whispered, "So who told everybody about the Ubvrdys, Abe."

"Hey, Jenny was in the library when I was looking up information for you. She was helping me with the periodical search file, that's all."

"Who asked you to find information for me? I'll do my own research. Just drop it!"

Trish had never talked to Abe that way. He was glad she turned away from him.

Abe talked to Eis after class and asked what Jenny had said that the class thought was so funny.

"She was bummed out to discover that she and Trish were doing the same report. She was typing her title and realized something was whacko. She looked up at the screen and saw her title in big capital letters and it said UBVRDY too. She was freaked because she had never heard of the Ubvrdy tribe before you told her about Trish's report. The kids were laughing because she thought she was under some kind of voodoo spell from Africa or something. But then she realized she had got her fingers on the wrong keys and that's why she typed ubvrdy. Trish's tribe didn't have anything to do with it."

"She got her fingers on the wrong keys? And it comes out the name of an African tribe? It is voodoo, Eis."

"Well hers wasn't really Ubvrdy. She said it was Ub-d-r-vy. It was really supposed to be Insect. Insect Camouflage, she said."

"I should have known. Jenny would think bugs are a critical mass. I think she identifies with them because she has bug eyes herself."

"Well it did sound pretty interesting, Abe."

"And what's the deal with Trish?" That was Abe's way of asking what Eis knew that he didn't.

"I'm not totally sure. She did talk some on the bus on Friday. She's just really upset about her report. Said it's been hard for her to decide on her topic. She's been a little touchy about it."

"Boy, I guess. So why doesn't she just do it on people wiping out the rain forests."

"I don't know. She knows what her critical mass is, but it's hard to do. Said she'll talk to Mr. R about it."

"Well, I could have told her there's not a thing in any of the encyclopedias about that Ubvrdy tribe," Abe said.

"That's the funny thing."

Abe waited, but Eis seemed to be lost in his own thoughts. "By a couple of things Trish said, I don't think it ever was about an African tribe."

"What?"

"I don't know."

They walked together down the hall, talking quietly, "She said if she does it on Ubvrdy, she'll do it by herself. Nobody would understand."

"Understand what?"

"I don't know. That's just what she said, man. I told her, 'Hey, Trish, this is Mr. Understanding Eisenhower at your service.' I stood up in the bus and bowed as I said it, and the bus driver yelled back that I had to sit down. But it didn't work anyway. Trish looked like she was about ready to cry and she said, 'I wish.' So what can you do when a girl does that? Say nothin' till she gets off the bus. I said, 'Bye, Trish.' She didn't say a word. Then this morning she was fine. Acted like nothing happened, but asked me to get the group to pass over her till she could okay working alone with Mr. R. That's it."

"So what's that all about?" Abe asked.

"Heck if I know. Come on, man, we'll be late for math."

"Yah. Don't worry about it." But what Abe really wanted to say was, don't get too involved, man.

Sometimes Abe wished Eis wasn't so funny, or that he was really ugly. And then he realized that it wouldn't matter if Eis were ugly, and that he was glad he was funny. He would like to have him engaged to Sara or something, or at least not talk to Trish so much. But at least Abe had never seen Trish wink at Eis.

Thoughts of Trish drifted away as he settled into math class and began comparing one of his homework problems to what was written on the board.

Abe steered clear of Trish the rest of that day and the next morning, except for a couple of questions she asked him in first period. By lunch he was missing her, but when she didn't show up in the cafeteria he was actually a little relieved. It was taking too much energy just to figure her out. He saved a corner at the lunch table for Eis, but he still hadn't come when Trevor and Ricardo finished their pizza and asked Abe if he wanted to go shoot hoops in the gym. Abe was glad somebody had invented basketball. It was a lot better thing to do than worry about girls—Trish or Maggie, for that matter.

Abe passed Mr. R's door on the way to basketball practice that afternoon, and saw that Trish was there. He went on by, not meaning to listen, but found his steps slowing. He caught Trish's voice saying, "I can do it. I want to. It is important. Thanks, Mr. R."

It sounded like she was getting ready to leave, but Abe didn't really feel like dealing with Trish even if she was in a better mood. He picked up his pace and was ready to turn the corner when he heard her voice behind him, "Hey, Abe, wait up." She ran down the hall to catch up and then continued, "My meeting with Mr. R didn't take as long as I thought. Think Mr. Speck would kick me out of the gym if I wait for Mom there?"

Abe knew Speck wouldn't care. Other kids sat on the bleachers by the door and watched practice sometimes. He also knew he should be excited that Trish wanted to watch. But he felt mixed up. What he really wanted to say was, "How can you talk to me now like nothing has happened when you've been yelling at me, treating me like junk. Why didn't you hurry up and catch the bus and tell all your troubles to Eis?"

But Trish cut into his thoughts, "No, never mind. I think I'll go to the library and see if I can get some stuff

Kathy Beckwith

for my essay." Trish sounded so normal. Abe couldn't figure her out. "So are you back on the Ubvrdy report?" he asked, and then instantly regretted having brought it up. Trish could explode again, and he didn't look forward to that.

Kathy Beckwith

Part II. TRISH

You think something is over. You try hard to make it all be over, and then one day, there it is, bigger than ever. That's how ubvrdy is for me.

Did you ever eat brussel sprouts? I think they're gross. But I can handle having one brussel on my plate with everything else. It sort of just becomes a part of dinner, and sometimes you can even ignore it and leave it on your plate. But what if somebody cooked one of those whole huge stems, about two feet long, covered all over with little brussels, and laid it across your plate and said that's it, that's your whole dinner? I wouldn't eat.

Well, sometimes ubvrdy is like that. It's too much. It starts to be everything. And I don't feel like eating.

—Trish

9

At dinner that night, Mrs. Carman mentioned Steve's phone call from Seattle and the various places the college choir would be singing over spring break.

"And what was that you were telling Steve about some hard class project, Trish?"

"It's our Critical Mass essay for Mr. R."

"Critical Mass? I thought Mr. R was your English teacher," Mr. Carman commented.

"He is."

"That's a physics term. What's critical mass got to do with English?"

"It just means it's something that's really important to us that we care a lot about right now and want to write on."

"Sounds good. So what are you writing on?" he asked as he scooped some rice and stir-fry into his mouth.

"What happened to us," Trish answered softly as she stared at the rice in the bowl in front of her. She could see the side of her dad's face stop chewing, but she didn't look up. The table was quiet for a long time. Mrs. Carman broke the silence, but her voice was barely audible, "What do you mean, Trish? About what?"

Trish was thinking about stir-fry as Mr. R pointed to his Quotation for the Day. Well, actually not the stir-fry, but how suddenly her dad's cheek had stopped chewing

Kathy Beckwith

it. It didn't fit together at all. Here Mr. R had been telling them to think of what is most important to them, really, and write about it. And then last night she had sat at the dinner table for almost an hour while her parents reminded her that she'd already dealt with this, that it's all finished, and she has to move on. They all have to move on, they had said, and that time will make it better. That she'll just hurt other people if she doesn't let it go.

She realized that Mr. R was setting the timer. "Nine minutes this time," he said, and everybody started writing. "Ms. Carman?" he questioned. She nodded her head yes and opened her journal.

"Hey, Abe," Trish whispered. "What are we supposed to be writing about? I thought he said we were done with our journals."

"Why we chose the topic we did," he answered. "Basically what we said in our small groups." And then he added coldly, "or should have said."

That's just what I mean, Trish thought to herself. Abe has no idea how impossible it is to talk about ubvrdy here. Nobody knows anything about it. And then she began writing:

"I guess I can't really write why I for sure chose ubvrdy as my topic, because I don't feel sure anymore. I don't think it's really essay material. But every time I think of doing it on something else, I feel like I'm chickening out. How am I supposed to figure it out? By the way, Mr. R, if you don't mind, could you stop reading here this once."

Trish put her arm up to the side of her paper to shield it somewhat should anyone glance her way, and then she continued.

"It's crazy that I'm thinking about this now, but I am, so there's nothing I can do about it. I believed two years ago that it wasn't any big deal, that I was okay. I told them that, and they were really happy. So happy. And they hugged me and everything. And my dad cried. But for some reason, I've started thinking about it again."

It was as if Trish's thoughts had been locked up behind a dam in her mind that broke and released them in a flood. Her pen flew across the page as she tried to keep up with them.

"I wonder what's going to happen when I love someone so much I start telling him everything. I wonder what's going to happen if I crack up some day and start crying in health class when they talk about being virgins. Am I supposed to pretend my whole life, to keep protecting other people. Or is it to protect me that I'm pretending? Pretending that ubvrdy never happened... never happens. I want to scream out to the whole wide world that nobody should ever be able to do this and that they should know that it's awful for a long, long time and they should have to think hard about it."

The words blurred when Trish wrote "think", so she went back and crossed out "think" and wrote in "cry". She stopped with that line and looked around the room. She let her face fall down on her sleeve to wipe the dampness from her eyes, and then looked up to see if

Kathy Beckwith

anyone was watching. The class was still writing. She went back to her paper and continued quickly.

"Actually I don't want people to know. Well, I don't know what I want. I just think people need somebody to tell them not to do it. I could do that. I really could. But I would cry."

Trish sat quietly, but shaking inside, waiting for the timer.

Mr. R asked them to hand their writing in when they left after class. Trish purposely stuffed hers into her notebook and looked the other way as she passed Mr. R's desk.

"Are you stopping by after class today, Ms. Carman?" he called out to her.

"I guess," she said quietly.

10

Trish took longer than usual at her locker, deciding if she wanted to go to the cafeteria. She hadn't brought a sack lunch, but she had a stash of crackers and an apple in her locker, and that would get her by. She didn't feel like doing a crowded lunchroom today. She needed some time to think about what she was going to say to Mr. R after school. Just as she reached up for the box of crackers, somebody yelled "Mouse!" behind her and stuck a finger in each side of her ribs.

"Eis! You nerd!"

The cracker box dropped to the floor and several fell out. Eis scooped them up and threw them into his mouth, adding, "Thanks, Trish. Is this lunch or hors d'oeuvres?"

"Lunch, I guess. I was just deciding if I wanted to eat in the cafeteria or go find some black hole to eat my crackers in."

"Definitely go for the black hole. Sounds so exciting that I think I'll go with you. My sack lunch could upgrade your crackers by six gingersnaps. Where are we headed?"

"We? Who said you were invited?"

"Eis Eisenhower is forever invited to whatever is happening in life. Right now I think it's your plan to escape the cafeteria. So let's go get sucked into the black hole." And then his tone changed and he looked

Kathy Beckwith

at Trish and added, "Unless you really mean it and you don't want me."

He made it sound so impossible and yet so serious that Trish knew she couldn't say no even if she didn't want Eis to come. It wasn't that important, just time to think, which couldn't happen with him there, she knew, but it seemed easier than sending him away, or going to the lunchroom. So she said, "Come on. Let's go to the side courtyard."

The horticulture class had taken the courtyard on as a project. It was pretty this time of year with the crocuses in bloom, and a few daffodils. It had a couple of park benches the construction class had made, but it still didn't get used very much because it was at the far end of the school, away from the lunchroom and the Snack Shack.

Trish was glad it was empty. Eis pulled out a sandwich and offered to tear off one side for her, but Trish said the crackers would be fine.

"So why the black hole attitude?" he asked.

"Sure, like I should tell you."

"Why not? We talk on the bus. You want me to bounce the bench around or something, so it feels like the bus?"

"No," Trish laughed. "I think you're tired of hearing about it, and I don't know how much more I can tell you anyway."

"Oh, ubvrdy again..." he said, looking at her sideways.

Trish knew she had talked too much already, that she had to work this out for herself. But she hadn't replied instantly, and Eis was soon chattering again.

"There is mysterious conflict boiling underneath the surface here, folks," he said, holding his fist up to his mouth to form a microphone. "We have a volcano ready to erupt, and this lady's telling us she's not leaving the mountain no matter what anyone says." He held the fist mike out to Trish, "Could you confirm that, Ma'am? Just speak into the mike."

"It's not funny, Eis."

He made some static sounds and then a loud squeal. "Darn. Mike must be too close to the amplifiers."

She pushed his hand away. "I just don't want you to look at me and see crap, that's all," she said quietly.

"Crap?" he questioned. "When did you start swearing?"

"That's not swearing."

"Not for people who say crap or shit all the time, but I thought you called it garbage or junk."

"This is different, Eis. This is crap."

"Okay. But just for the record, I guarantee I will never see you as crap. You're cool, and I like you a lot," he said seriously. "Oh, don't take that wrong," he added quickly. "I'm not trying to bust up things with Lewis or steal winks or anything."

Eis quickly reached up and slapped his hands over his ears.

"What's wrong?" Trish asked.

"Nothing. Just my ears turn hot every once in a while, when I say the wrong thing. I heard that elephants have big ears to cool them down. Their blood rushes to their ears when they get stressed out, and the air takes the heat out. God tried the same trick when He made people, but He forgot and made little ears. It doesn't work. Mine just catch on fire and turn bright red. Does that happen to girls too?"

"Not to me, but I don't know about girls in general," Trish answered.

Eis finished his sandwich. "Gingersnaps?" he offered.

"Thanks."

"Should I have just stopped with the crap?" he finally asked.

"Don't you dare take back one word you said. You're cool too, Eis. And you know my winks are just for Abe."

For just a second Trish wondered why she had let Eis come, why she had even let him know she felt like a black hole. She couldn't do that with Abe. For Abe, she wanted to seem good. She wanted him to believe in her, to trust her. She wanted him to want her. Someday she wanted him really close to her. She couldn't tell him anything about this. But Eis was safe somehow. Like Steve would be. Or he had just been there at the right time and made a black hole seem okay, and he didn't go away.

Trish stared at the bed of crocuses in front of them. There was a little metal sign that read "Mayfield High Timberwolf," but the design hadn't worked. She had never been able to see a wolf head in the flowers. It didn't matter. She thought they were good enough just to bloom.

She rolled her apple around in her hand and then said, "Eis, I want to tell you about Mrs. Kratzer, an old lady who volunteers at the library with my mom."

"Sure, change the subject entirely," he said. "I love a good story."

"This isn't changing the subject. It's a true story and it has a point," Trish added.

"Okay, you're on."

"Well," she began, "there's this lady, Mrs. Kratzer, who is in the Friends of the Library group with my mom—a regular old lady, white hair, kind of little, nice. She and my mom were working at our house sorting some books for a sale they were having and my mom says she has to go to the bathroom and she'll be right back. Well, I know they're boxing books by what age group would like what, so I offer to help, and when mom comes back, Mrs. Kratzer..."

Here Trish stopped a minute and looked right at Eis. "I'm not sure you'll like this part, but it's important to the story."

"Of course, I love it. This is just like a Louis L'Amour. I'm all ears." And then he added, "And they're not even hot."

Trish continued, "Anyway, my mom comes back and asks Mrs. Kratzer if she wants to take a break, meaning does she want a drink or something. And Mrs. Kratzer says No, she already went to the bathroom since it was Saturday. I guess she assumed Mom meant a bathroom break. Anyway, my mom and I both stop dead in our tracks and stare at her, and Mrs. Kratzer sort of giggles and says, 'Well, you know what I mean, really go.'

"I didn't exactly know what she meant, but I decided to keep sorting books for a while and she starts telling my mom this incredible story that she had been a teacher for forty years and that she was so busy during the week that she never could take the time to 'sit on the bathroom,' she called it, so she just got used to storing it up. 'Storing it up.' Those were her exact words, Eis. Until Saturday morning. Then she said she'd relax and 'go' for the week. No lie, Eis.

"She said she even went to a doctor once because she was worried about not being regular, and she wondered if she should start drinking prune juice, and the doctor said she could but it seemed that that was her regular and not to worry about it. She just kept looking down at her books and sorting them into boxes the whole time, like it was normal every day conversation. I gave my mom a 'what-is-this-dork?' look, and she threw me a 'quiet-Trish-it's-okay' look in return. Later on I asked Mom if anybody could hold a week's supply of poop and if a doctor would really say it was okay, and she said 'Beats me. I've never tried...or asked.' And we just laughed.

"Is this too gross, Eis?" Trish questioned.

"No. No, I hear crap every day!"

Trish continued, "But the thing is, I've seen Mrs. Kratzer maybe ten times since then, and every time I see her, I don't think of an oldish lady with white hair or even a lady who sorts books. I mentally make a note of how many days we have since the last Saturday, and if it's Friday, I mental math that she's 6/7 full of crap, and if it's Tuesday she's 3/7 full of crap. I can tell you any day of the week. Try me."

Eis was getting into the story, and quipped, "Thursday." Trish gave a quiz team reply: "5/7 full of crap."

"Monday."

"2/7 full of crap." They laughed. "I think of her as a walking crap bank, Eis. And all because she told that one dumb story she could have kept to herself. Should have kept to herself. Because nobody's any better off because she told. It doesn't make any difference now that it's done. So that's the point, Eis."

"That's the point, huh... Of course." Then in his Mr. R voice he added, "Would you clarify the point of your crappy story, Ms. Carman?"

It brought a smile to Trish's solemn face. "I know it's totally crazy," she said, "but it exactly applies to me."

Now it was Eis's turn to smile. "Hey, Trish, take a break. I mean if you need to 'go,' then just pretend it's Saturday."

She slapped at his shoulder. "No, you dummy. It has nothing to do with the bathroom. The point is..." She paused and then continued softly, "It's ubvrdy, Eis. It's my ubvrdy. And I'm afraid it matters now. It's starting to be a critical mass for me and I didn't want it to be. They said it didn't have to be, but it is."

"Hey, hold on, Trish. You have lost me way back in the depths of the jungle. Is we talkin' African tribes here or library ladies going to the john once a week?"

"Neither, Eis."

"Well, in that case you're going to have to talk louder or draw me a picture. I missed the message."

"Okay. I'll back up a little. It's like I said. If people know, they may just look at me and see crap, automatically just think about what happened when I was little." She looked at Eis and knew he still didn't understand, so she continued.

"Eis, I went to a counselor for almost two years after Dad went back East. It's not like there's nobody who understands. It's just that sometimes it feels like the world that understands is some other secret world, and my world, my friends, the people I really talk to, don't know me, Eis. Don't know what suddenly comes into my mind for no good reason. Don't know how much I hate it. Don't know me at all. And I worry now that if they did, it wouldn't be okay. And that when I find somebody, maybe somebody like Abe, who really matters forever, it won't be okay at all."

"Hey, what's there to know, Trish? Smart girl, 7 foot 11 $\frac{1}{2}$ inches tall, 685 pounds."

"Eis!" she protested his description of her, then suddenly became serious again. "Eis, I'm older now. I've been thinking about this a lot lately, thinking that maybe it matters more than they told me it does. That maybe it's going to matter for the whole rest of my life. Mr. R telling us to get in touch with our Critical Mass didn't help any. Or maybe it did. Anyway, I finally decided I'd talk to him about it. But he's still not one of us.

"Eis, I just want kids to see me as Trish, as me..." She paused a moment before finishing the sentence, "not as somebody who's been... not as what happened when I was Daddy's little princess."

The look in Trish's eyes betrayed the fact that it had slipped out, or that she at least suddenly regretted having said it, that she wanted to take her words back, even from Eis. Tears sprang into her eyes and she quickly wiped them away, but when they wouldn't be gone, she buried her face in her arms.

Trish couldn't look up, even when Eis asked quietly, "What happened when you were your Daddy's little princess? What are you talking about?"

She didn't answer.

"Something about that princess dress again? What's going on, Trish?" But now she didn't really feel that he was asking her. Maybe he understood he'd have to figure it out himself, because she couldn't say the words.

Then she barely heard, "Oh, no... God, no..." as if he were pleading for her to stop his thoughts and tell another story.

"Trish, that's not true, is it?" he asked as he pulled her face up to look in her eyes. She didn't answer, but couldn't keep from biting her lip while the tears streamed down her cheeks.

"That happens to somebody whose old man is a jerk, a drunkard or something," he continued, "not somebody who makes chili beans and prays and jokes around about Macbeth videos. God, Trish! Is this some bad joke?"

Trish saw that tears had filled her friend's eyes too.

"Why do people do crazy, awful things to their own kids?" he asked. But as if he didn't expect an answer, he reached out and picked up her hand and held it. It seemed to Trish that they sat there together for a long time, and then he spoke again. "I understand, Trish. I do understand."

She looked right at him, and questioned, "And you don't think I'm awful or dirty?"

"No," was his simple reply. And then he added, "It's just like I said, Trish. You're cool."

"Thank you, Eis," she said through the tears.

11

"I should have just turned it in after class," Trish said to Mr. R, handing him her journal sheet as she walked into the room.

"That's okay, Trish. Won't you sit down while I read it?" He automatically reached for one of the red markers in his pencil holder, but he didn't use it. He just twirled it around in his hand as he started reading.

"Do you want me to read on?" he asked after the first few sentences.

"Sure," Trish answered. "I know I said not to read it, but it's okay now. I want to talk to you about it."

He read on. Slowly, it seemed to Trish. When he looked up at her, Trish noticed he was biting his lip, and then she let her eyes fall down to the desktop. Maybe she shouldn't have. Maybe Mr. R couldn't help her anyway.

"Trish..." he said, and waited for her to look at him. "I understand now what you meant. I'm sorry. I am sorry. This has been a hard project for you."

"It's okay, Mr. R" she said automatically, and then a little laugh caught in her throat. "No," she said, "I don't mean that. It's not okay. I know that now. And that's why I'm here."

"Go on, Trish," he encouraged.

"When you started talking about the Critical Mass essay, I knew. I knew from the beginning. It's time for me to say something, Mr. R, or to do something that will tell people this is not okay."

"It was your dad, then?" he asked. Trish nodded her head yes. "Have you talked with a counselor, Trish?" he added.

"A lot. The two years my dad was gone till part way through eighth grade. Then I thought I was doing okay. Mom said she thought we could quit. She thought it was time to finally put it all behind us."

"And what did you think, Trish?"

"Sounded good to me. I just wanted to be normal. I didn't ever want to think about it again. But after a while it started to come back. I know it sounds totally crazy, Mr. R, but a boy kissed me. I wanted him to. And then I freaked. Over a kiss. I started thinking about things all over again and wondering about things."

Mr. R didn't answer, but his eyes told Trish that he was with her.

"Things like what will happen when there's somebody I'm ready to love and they find out about this. And what kids would think of me if they knew. Or maybe they do know already, and don't say anything, but just think I'm weird. And what if I start crying someday in health class for no reason... Oh, I guess I wrote that in my journal."

"That's okay, Trish."

"And why people think it should be kept a secret when the whole world needs to know and somebody needs to yell at them so they'll never do it again."

"Is it a secret, Trish?"

"Well, it wasn't, really, at first, totally. After Mom found out. But now it seems like it is again. Actually, it was in some newspaper when I was in 6th grade. Not my name, I mean, but Dad's, and it said he was convicted of something. I know a few people in our church knew because they told my mom not to get a divorce. The judge let Dad go to a sex-offender treatment place back East that they knew was good.

"But, Mr. R, besides Steve, no other kid ever talked to me. Not one of my friends ever said anything. Anything. I think maybe nobody told the kids. And I know a lot of people at church just thought Dad's job got transferred back East because that's what they said.

"My counselor knows, and Dad's counselor and probation officer, but now that I don't go anymore, that doesn't really count. It's like it's all turned back into an awful secret again. And you can't say a word. Like you wonder about things, but it's not supposed to be a big deal anymore. Like it's your fault for thinking about it."

She paused, and then added, "Nobody in my world knows, Mr. R."

"And do you want your world to know?"

"No. I mean, yes. Yes, I do. I want to be done wondering what will happen if somebody finds out. How they'll act the next time they see me. What they'll say. I'm sick of the wondering. I want them all to know." And then she added quietly, "And then forget it for the rest of their lives. Besides..." But she stopped without finishing the sentence.

"Besides what, Trish?"

"Besides, if the boys knew... I mean if they really knew the whole story, they'd make sure they never did it. They'd read books on how to not abuse somebody. It would be a big deal and people would talk about it. If they knew how bad my mom cried, and Steve. If they knew what it was like for me, how I hated to see him come into my room. How I hated to have him look at me. How I never wanted anyone to look at me. How I cried and cried in my pillow so nobody would hear. How bad I wish it could never have happened."

And then the words tumbled out, "Mr. R, I don't know if you know anything about this or not, but I've read a lot of books and articles and stuff, down at the library, and I know that boys do this even before they get married and have their own little girls. They do this to their cousins and their sisters. And it's not always weirdos who got raped or beat up when they were little. Sometimes it's just guys who think it won't matter.

"Or girls. Girls can hurt kids too. I guess nobody tells them how awful it all ends up. Nobody ever talks about what it's really like."

Trish paused and spoke softly when she said, "Like sometimes it's regular fathers, that you love, Mr. R It gets all mixed up."

"Yes, it does, Trish."

And she continued, "If kids who are thinking about doing this only knew what really happens they'd be the ones to cry in health class if anybody would talk about it for real."

Mr. R put his fist up over his mouth, like he does when he's thinking, and just stared beyond Trish for a moment. "We don't talk about it much, do we, Trish? I guess a lot of people don't know what to do or say."

He paused and then continued, "I wonder, Trish, if there are two stories here. I don't know. I'm just wondering. Is one the ubvrdy...?"

He didn't finish, but broke into his own thought. "Trish, where in the world did that word come from? Did you make it up?"

She smiled. "No. I'm as bad a typist as Jenny. Remember when she told about typing *Insect* and it came up *Ubvrdy*? Or actually, *ubdrvy*. I never thought my secret word would be decoded by Jenny's typing mistake. I started it by accident about a year ago, when I got my fingers on the wrong keys. Then it seemed a good way to be a little bit brave. I could move all my fingers over one space, right together in the middle of the keyboard, like I did on accident, and type it so I never had to see the other word. It always came out "ubvrdy". Try it on your computer sometime. Then I could write about what happened, just to myself, on my computer, and then delete it."

"So that's it," he said, smiling. And then he continued, "Well, what I'm wondering is, if there are two stories. One is yours, the ubvrdy, that is personal and difficult and confusing to talk about or write about. The other is incest—sex between relations, or just sexual abuse in general, and I wonder if that's the thing you want to talk about now."

She was surprised that he said it right out loud in a normal voice. Incest. She had been saying "ubvrdy" in her mind for so long that the word "incest" seemed strange. But she was glad he had. She wanted to say it too.

"But you can't separate ubvrdy and incest, Mr. R. They're the same thing. They're what happened to me. They're what my dad did to me, over and over again."

"I'm sorry, Trish. I wish that had never happened. Maybe you're right. Maybe they can't be separated. Maybe they shouldn't be separated. I don't know. But there are people speaking out against sexual abuse who have never experienced it."

"High school kids?"

"Probably. I know that my nephew and some scouts from his troop took a video program about sexual abuse prevention to a group of churches in Salem. It's something they watched at one of their meetings, and decided to offer as a service project. That probably took some courage.

"And there was an article in our teacher's journal recently about a group of high schoolers that challenged their school board to come up with an abuse prevention program after one of their teachers was arrested for sexual abuse of a student. Eventually, the school board and the students worked together and developed a program for their elementary and middle schools, and a forum they do every year at the high school. So those kids are involved. I don't know if they include protection against incest, but it would make sense."

Trish sat for a long time, but she was thinking.

"I've been wanting to do something, Mr. R. On and off for a long time. But I didn't think I could. It would get too mixed up with me and Dad and Mom. Now ever since our Critical Mass project started, I can't get rid of the thought that I've got to do something. That this is the time."

Doubt showed on her face as she continued, "Even if I did it generally, what would I say if anyone asks why it's a critical mass for me?"

"I have a hunch you'd come up with an answer that's okay for you, Trish."

"Will they even care about it, the other kids?"

"I think some of them will, a lot. There are probably some here who have been through it too."

Trish found that a strange thought.

"Some of them wouldn't believe it could ever happen to them or anyone they knew," he continued, "so they wouldn't care as much. But because they don't know, don't believe it, doesn't mean it's not happening."

"I know that, Mr. R."

"A few might make something hurtful out of it, but I would hope not. I think a lot of them would understand that it's something that happens that must be changed. I don't know. Like you said, it isn't talked about very much.

"I don't know how kids would react, Trish. I wish I could tell you for sure. But I will tell you this, for sure. If it is critical to you, and you want to write your essay on it and do the presentation, I'm with you."

"Thanks, Mr. R." She paused, and sat thinking for a while. "I think what is critical is that I do something, just so maybe one person won't have ubvrdy to live through. Incest or sexual abuse of any kind, I mean. I think that's what's bothering me most, Mr. R. That I know about it, but that I haven't done anything to make people stop. I think I can talk about incest, Mr. R, and maybe leave ubvrdy for now." Then Trish added, "Except I already told Eis. That was dumb."

"You've talked to Eis about this?"

"Just today, at lunch. I just couldn't keep it inside any longer, and he came along. My folks will freak. Telling a teacher and a friend in the same day, after it's been such a secret. They don't understand, Mr. R. They don't know what it's like." Trish looked down at her fingernails to keep down the hurt in her throat. She didn't want to cry in front of him.

"Have you talked to them recently, Trish?"

"Yes. It ruined our dinner. I think they're scared. Like they can't control what I'll say and it might wreck everything for them if I tell. Like they still have friends that would never believe my dad could have done that. And they don't want them to know. That knowing won't do any good. It'll only hurt more. And I know why they say that.

"But the thing is, Mr. R, we're just keeping the lie going. Like a man can do that to his little girl and she'll be fine and nobody has to say anything, and then some other man can do that and nobody will say anything." She paused and looked right at Mr. R. "I'm not fine, Mr.

R. Not today. And the only thing I can think of now to get finer, I mean better, is to make it all stop."

Trish felt shaky and knew she couldn't go on, or she would cry. She waited for Mr. R to say something.

"Don't you think they want it to stop too, Trish, your parents?"

"I know my mom would. And my dad should. He acted like he was sorry. Except..."

"Except what?"

"Except for something I've been thinking about."

Mr. R waited, and Trish continued, "He said once... No, not once. He said a lot of times that my mom probably didn't mind if he did it to me because she got too tired at night and he wanted sex more than she did. That if she did know she probably wouldn't care, she'd just share him with me. I remember that. And another time he said there wouldn't be anything wrong with it if people didn't think it was wrong. Wasn't he gentle? he asked. He didn't hurt me, did he? he asked. "Didn't it feel good, baby?"

"Gol, I can't believe I'm telling you this. Can you imagine that, Mr. R? Like if he's gentle it's okay. Like he can use me up because my mom doesn't want sex and it's okay and it's other people's fault that we thought it was a big deal."

Trish's voice had picked up a tone of anger, and she continued, "That's what's crap, Mr. R! Pardon the expression. And I never told a soul about that till right now. I never told Mom. I never told my counselor. I never even told my brother, Steve, that he said that.

"Why didn't I tell anybody that, Mr. R? Was I afraid it was true? I mean, am I a sick-o or something, that I think a man can rape his daughter because he wants sex and his wife doesn't? I really think my dad's a sick-o. Or else why would he say stuff like that? But he's not some freak, Mr. R. He really isn't. And he hasn't touched me for years. He doesn't even give me a hug.

"But that's crazy, isn't it? A woman doesn't have to have sex to keep her husband from getting his little girl, does she?"

"No, Trish. It doesn't work that way."

"I know. But I remember thinking that when I grew up I'd want sex all the time so it would never happen to my little girl. But then I'd think that I'd never want sex and so what would happen to her then? And now I wished I had told my mom what he said and it would have made her yell at him instead of just cry. Then he'd know he can't say stuff like that. But instead I was a chicken or something. And now I think she'd stick up for him. Or it would be my fault if she got mad at him again.

"I know one thing now. I'm never having kids, or better yet, I'll never ever get married, and I'll never have sex and I'll scream if anybody ever suggests it, and then my husband will rape me, and awwkk.... Mr. R, I'm going crazy!"

"I can tell that, Trish," he smiled gently. "But that's okay. You can go crazy. And you can talk about all this. I don't exactly feel like a genius in this area, Trish. It might not be a bad idea to look your counselor up again."

"My folks would disown me."

"Really? Don't you think you could talk to them about what you need now? About what you want to do now?"

"They'd get mad. Or maybe really sad. It's hard to talk to somebody if those are your two choices."

"Trish, I don't know, but I bet there have been other times through all this when somebody's been mad or really sad, and you've worked through it together. It's hard for anybody to go back to something they thought they had finished, especially something hard. And this must be hard for your folks too. But that doesn't mean they can't help you, or that they won't help you if they know you need it. They may have times when it all comes back to them too. I hear that happens with things like this. It comes circling back when you don't expect it."

"I don't know. It just seems so mixed up. Why did he do it in the first place, Mr. R? Why did I let him? Why didn't I hit him? Why didn't I tell Mom the first time he touched me?" Trish didn't mean for the tears to come, but she couldn't hold them back any longer. Her eyes filled and blurred, and she bit her lip to make it stop shaking.

"Why am I asking the same things I already asked my counselor and we talked about a bajillion times? Why did he ask me if it felt good? Oh, that is so gross!

Forget I ever said that, Mr. R. I hate it. I hate it! I am so sick of all this stuff coming back in my head.

"Will it ever, ever be over?" she pleaded.

"I don't know, Trish, but you'll make it. I know you will," he answered.

She sat there for a while until it didn't hurt so much to breathe. She took a tissue from her pocket and wiped her face.

"You know, Mr. R, I got my license the day after Thanksgiving. That very same Saturday I backed the car into a tree at the side of our driveway. It broke out the taillight and crunched the whole corner. Dumb. I can't believe I did it. And you know what he said, my dad? 'Those things happen. We'll get it fixed.' I was so relieved I started crying, and so he says, I think just to make me feel better, 'It's time we got some of that insurance money back.'

"I nodded my head yes. He could have made me pay for it, Mr. R, and that would have been fair, but he just had me practice backing up. I know that's not important, but he's nice. And he was nice before too. It's like if you heard that this person who plays the most beautiful piano music in the whole world is really a psycho killer or something. Something that doesn't go together. I don't understand it. My dad sweeps spiders up and tosses them outside instead of stepping on them. I could have grown up thinking that's what you do with spiders, except my mom smashes them. He goes hiking. He plays guitar and tells somewhat funny jokes. He had our family sponsor a little boy from Guatemala so he could have supplies and money to pay for school. And that was all happening at the same time he was…"

She was quiet. "I really don't understand it, Mr. R."

Trish's voice made a couple of hiccup sounds. She laughed at herself, then just sat there. She took in a deep breath, rolled her shoulders, and let out a heavy sigh.

"You know what, Mr. R?" she said. "This is my Critical Mass topic. I will do it. I don't know about ubvrdy, or about me and Dad and Mom, or what we're going to do, or if tomorrow I'll wish I wouldn't have told Eis… or you. But I do know one thing right now. I'm doing my essay on incest. And I'm going to make a great presentation, and because of my presentation somebody's not going to get hurt. I don't know who. But somebody. I can do it. I want to. It is important. Thanks, Mr. R!"

Whether or not he was going to say something else, he didn't have a chance. Trish gathered her papers and turned for the door. She looked over her shoulder on her way out, and added, "Thanks a lot, Mr. R. You know, you're pretty cool."

Kathy Beckwith

Part III. ABE

There's this place on the way back from Idaho that's pretty steep. So steep that there are warning signs everywhere and a brake test area, mostly for the big trucks. And there's this truck ramp, so that if your brakes go out and you're out of control, the runaway truck can swerve up a gravel ramp and stop instead of going pell-mell, crashing into something.

I wonder if there'll be a truck ramp for me if I decide I want it. Sometimes I get the feeling that the brakes are going out and the hill is steeper than I realized. Or that it's too late for brakes or escape ramps, and what I have to do instead is just let go, feel the rush, and not even think about brakes. Especially if at the bottom of the hill somebody else had a great ride too.

And they will, or they would have told you to check the brakes.

—Abe

12

Trish didn't explode. "You mean my essay topic?" she answered Abe. "Ubvrdy's out. I'm doing it on something else."

"You don't need to tell me," Abe quickly added as they walked together down the hallway. He thought maybe there was still time to change the subject.

"No, that's okay. It's no big secret." Trish paused a moment, then said firmly, "I'm doing it on incest."

The breath rushed out of Abe's mouth and he stopped dead in his tracks. He stood staring at Trish's back. She turned around and faced him. Abe tried to read her eyes, but she looked normal.

"What?" she said.

"Nothing." He couldn't think of anything to say. What he was really thinking was, how in the world did you come up with incest on the spur of the moment? He knew Trish must be embarrassed to tell him the name of her topic, but she was doing a pretty good cover up. They turned down the hall toward the library. "I thought you were going to basketball, Abe."

"I am." He wheeled around and walked the other way. "See ya later."

"See ya, Abe."

He went a few steps, then suddenly turned back into the hallway going to the library. It was empty, except for Trish.

"Trish..." he called.

"Yeah?"

Kathy Beckwith

And the words came out, not because he had thought about what he was saying, but because he wanted to know, "Do you know anything about it... incest?"

"I'll research it, Abe." and she pulled the library door open. "See ya."

"Okay."

Their week of research went quickly. Abe talked to Ms. Stewart, the librarian. She recommended some articles, then told him about a friend of hers who was proud of fighting in Korea and a teacher who headed for Canada during the Vietnam War. He could interview them.

"What teacher was that?" Abe asked. His mind had drifted, wondering who Ms. Stewart would suggest Trish interview about incest.

Would Trish be embarrassed to say it was a Critical Mass topic for her, especially since it was something she really didn't know anything about. And then a funny thought hit him. How's she going to make her class presentation on this and who would ever agree to work with her on it?

Part of Abe's question was answered the next day during first period. The Quotation for the Day was written on one half of the board, and on the other side was a list of all the Critical Mass topics that had been selected. Abe first looked for his own, War, and then glanced to see if Incest was there. It was, right above Jenny's Insect Camouflage. Mr. R asked the class to look at the list to make sure their topic was there. Then he wanted them to give a little thought to a second topic they could help present.

Jenny's voice rang out, "Wow, Mr. R, somebody else is doing Insects. We're partners for sure without thinking!" Several kids started laughing, so Jenny corrected herself. "I mean, we'll think a lot, but we have to be partners for sure."

Mr. R turned to Trish, "Well, Ms. Carman, I don't know if you can resist such enthusiasm from classmate Radke, but I will point out a small difference in spelling, Miss Radke."

He walked to the board and underlined the c's and the s's in the words and then continued "...so that you will be aware of the fact that you will be helping Ms. Carman with her presentation on Incest, not Insects."

"Incest!?" Jenny's voice started so high and squeaky as she repeated the word, that when she wrinkled her face and crossed her eyes, Abe couldn't help but laugh out loud. So did most of the class, including Trish. Any feeling of anger Trish had toward Jenny the other day, seemed to be melting away, as Jenny rambled on, "Sure, Trish, I'll do great role plays on incest, I mean, you know, not on the actual incest itself, but on what your report about it says is cool, I mean not what is cool about incest but..." Jenny crossed her eyes again and slid down into her desk. Then she turned to Trish and said, "I'd love to work with you, Trish, but next time could we do something easy like your African tribe or my bugs?"

"Sure, Jenny." Trish seemed to relax. She looked at Abe and he thought for a moment she had winked. How nice to have her back, even if she did have a crazy essay to work on.

13

Abe stood in line in the cafeteria. For ravioli. He was borderline on gagging over ravioli, and figured it wasn't worth waiting for, but he hated the idea that there wouldn't be anything more to eat until after basketball practice, and his stomach would growl all afternoon. He planned to check the lunch menu ahead of time so he could bring a sack lunch when it was something awful like ravioli, but he never remembered. He saw Trish come through the door and waved to her to cut in line with him.

"Yum, ravioli," she said.

"You don't like ravioli," Abe said, and then he caught her wink.

"Of course not. But I like to watch you eat it."

They picked up their trays and headed for the table where Eis, Trevor, and Sara were sitting. Abe spotted Eis's sack lunch, and said, "Hey, there's hope. I'll trade you ravioli for any one lunch item, Eis."

Eis unpacked a sandwich and four gingersnaps and set them in front of him. "You wouldn't want them, man. I spit on them before I put them in the sack."

"You what?" It was Sara.

"I spit on them."

"You mean 'spat,' man," corrected Trevor. "It goes spit, spat, sput."

"Okay, man, I spit spat sput on them before I put them in the sack. I'm not going to risk losing my lunch on a ravioli day."

"You bluffer," Sara called out. She snatched a gingersnap and popped it into her mouth. Eis reached over, took the French bread off her tray, spat on it, and set it down in front of him.

"Okay," Sara said, "you can have my bread."

The talk turned to movies at the local theater. One was a cartoon rated G and the other was "Well Water" with Kayler Jordan. Trevor said he'd already seen it, but he'd go again if they went during economy hour, that it was a great story about the California Gold Rush days.

"What's the rating?" Trish asked.

"I forget. But it has a bit of skin and a little action in bed. Probably R."

"Then I'm out," Trish said, "even if I could get in. My folks are on this protective kick. They have to see the movie first and decide if it has any merit."

Good, thought Abe. He had seen a couple of Kayler Jordan movies with Eis, then rented them again to see by himself. He wasn't sure he could sit next to Trish, watching "a little action in bed."

"Let's just do something else," Sara said.

"Like what?" Trevor asked.

"Like what we used to do before we started going to movies so much," replied Trish.

"We didn't do anything before we started going to the movies. Unless your youth group had something going on."

Abe knew Trevor was right. Most of them had known each other for years, but it wasn't until last year when Zach came as Youth Pastor to their church that some of the kids got started doing things together.

"I had a Twister party in 3rd grade," Trish said. "I still have the plastic mat."

"I still have mine too," Sara said.

"Okay, we could have a Double Twister party. Whoopee. What else do I have to choose from?" Trevor asked.

"S'mores in my fireplace," Sara added.

They were soon competing for the best idea—laser tag, miniature golf, foosball tournament, karaoke.

"How about a bike ride?" Abe asked.

"Sounds good, except my bike has two flat tires," Sara answered.

"Maggie has a bike you can borrow," Abe volunteered.

"Tires can be fixed, Sara," Trevor said. "Where do you ride, Abe?"

"Out past the Grange. Then there are a couple different places you can go."

"Is that out by Mint Creek where we had our 4th grade field trip?" Trevor asked.

"Fourth grade!" Eis interjected. "You guys have known each other since 4th grade?"

"Longer than that. Except Sara was in the other class. They had their own field trip," Trevor replied.

"Well, Sara, looks like you and I missed out on something really big. How 'bout we get them to take us on a science field trip to Mint Creek this Saturday? Maybe we can catch some tadpoles."

"Hey, you really can, Eis," Trevor answered. "I got some that stayed alive for almost a year. They turned into little water frogs, but their tank smelled so bad my mom dumped them out."

"Bummer," Trish commented.

"Not really. I forgot to feed them. They'd been dead for a couple of weeks."

"Trevor!"

It was agreed they'd meet Saturday afternoon at Abe's house.

14

"Sara?" Maggie asked. "You're going riding with Sara? What is this switcheroo with Eis business? I thought you liked Trish."

"Maggie, I asked for your bike, not for an interrogation."

"Maybe."

"Maybe what?"

"Maybe you can let Sara use my bike, if..."

"If what?"

"If you tell me all about your love life and if Trish is nice to you and what you think about her, and how it feels to have somebody you knew since kindergarten become a girlfriend, and what you do."

"You are insane, Maggie! I don't have such a thing as a love life, and I wouldn't be blackmailed into telling you if I did. Trish happens to be coming too."

But Maggie just smiled and said, "Okay, Abe, Sara can use my bike, since I have to vacuum the house anyway, and I'll wait to hear about your love life till you get one."

Abe shook his head. Maggie couldn't lose. He felt a bit disgusted with her. But it was nice to know she thought about such questions. He'd like to talk to somebody about what it's like to have known Trish for so long and now have the funny feeling that you know her in a whole different way, a way you hoped might happen.

He hadn't told anybody that they had kissed. Once, a couple of months ago. It wasn't his favorite memory. He had thought about kissing Trish for a long time, and then one day it just happened. They had gone for a walk on the hiking trails along the creek behind the library. Trish had crouched down to see a little newt moving under the edge of some leaves, and as she stood, Abe offered her a hand. It had happened so gently, her rising into his arms, their eyes meeting, their lips touching, softly, purposefully.

Abe would have held her, for a long time, but she pulled away, roughly, and said, "Where'd it go?" as if the newt were suddenly important. The gentleness turned to embarrassment. Abe wondered if he did something wrong. It felt like the time he leapt out to catch a Frisbee and landed on a bee barefooted. Suddenly stung, for no reason, when he had just made a beautiful catch.

Eis pulled up in his dad's pickup with Trevor and Trish beside him and three bikes in the back. Sara rode up as they were unloading the bikes, and Maggie soon realized that they had four bikes for four people.

"Hey, Abe, Sara doesn't need my bike after all."

"No," Sara replied, "Eis came over and we fixed both my tires."

"So maybe I should go along," Maggie offered.

"Sure" they all answered. But Abe knew they misunderstood Maggie. She wasn't asking for their permission. She didn't stop to think that she might not be wanted. She was trying to figure out if she could do the ride and still get the vacuuming done before Mom got home from her workshop. Abe wished Maggie would have asked him, but she didn't.

"This will work. Hey, if you guys can pedal slow, I'll go get my helmet and call Gabi. We'll catch up with you before the Grange."

Abe would have protested, but Trish was already answering, "We're not in that big of a hurry, Maggie. Call Gabi. We'll wait." She ran into the house to make the call, and within minutes the entourage of seven was headed for Mint Creek.

They didn't have much luck searching for tadpoles. "Probably so much pollution in the creek that the frogs are dying out," Trish commented.

"Either that, or it's not tadpole season," Trevor added. Since no one knew if and when there was a tadpole season, they left the tadpole idea and walked up the creek to where Abe thought he had remembered an old beaver dam. Whether the creek had changed or they were at the wrong place, Abe didn't know. What they found was a big tree that had fallen and created a walkway over the creek to an outcropping of rocks on the other side. Eis swung his backpack off his shoulder and, bringing out a bag of cookies, said, "Anybody for a gingersnap?"

"Great idea, Eis. Let's go have cookies on the rocks, Gabi!" It was Maggie. She had scooped his bag of gingersnaps away and was doling out a handful to each person.

"Hey, Maggie, try for two points." Trevor opened his mouth as wide as he could and was challenging Maggie to make a basket.

"Let's play HORSE, Maggie," Gabi quipped, and she tossed one of her gingersnaps toward Trevor's open mouth. It smacked him on the ear instead.

"Watch it, Gabi!" Trevor said as he picked up the cookie and put it in his mouth.

"Oops. That's H for me," Gabi laughed. "Your turn, Maggie."

"No way. Basketball's over. Let's play hockey," Trevor suggested as he raised both arms to guard his face.

"But basketball's your critical mass, Trevor," Trish said, lopping one of her cookies at him.

"At least it's a little more fun than insect incest," he joked back as he caught the cookie and popped it into his mouth.

Abe looked up to catch Trish's reaction. He wished Trevor had not mentioned the subject. It was Saturday in the woods. No need to bring up school now, but Trish didn't seem upset.

It was Maggie's response that got their attention. "I didn't think insects worried about incest, Trevor. I thought they just mated with whoever was around."

"God, Maggie!" It was Abe. He could almost see her lips start to form the words, "We don't talk like that, Abe," but instead she was back to the topic.

"Is it instinct or something? I mean, if they hatch out a thousand eggs at a time, how are they supposed to know who their relatives are?" and then she slowed down a little and looked around sheepishly. "Oops. It was a joke. You're not really doing a report on insect incest, are you?" she asked Trish.

"No, Maggie, just regular incest."

"Really? Oh, that ought to be easier."

This time Abe said his "God, Maggie," under his breath. He didn't even know she knew what incest was. And here she was telling Trish that incest would be an easy report. She was totally insane. Too insane for words.

"You know, Trish," Maggie rambled, "there's this lady from India that gave a talk in our World Cultures class last month. She might have some neat stuff for your report. Don't you think, Gabi? Remember what she said about marriages?"

"No doubt!" Gabi said. "She told us about how most parents arrange the marriages for the kids instead of just letting them fall in love with just anybody, and we almost freaked when she said sometimes a girl hopes her uncle is the one they'll get to marry her, because then she knows that her mother-in-law will be nice to her and not mean and make her do all the work like they do sometimes."

"Because, see, you get why, Trish?" Maggie interrupted. "She goes to live with her husband's family. And this way the mother-in-law is her own grandma, who already loves her. Isn't that funny?

"But then this kid in our class asked if there wasn't some law against incest, and she said, 'Of course there is. Every culture has laws against incest.' But she didn't seem to get the point, which was if some uncle here did something, you know, weird like, to his niece, they'd throw him into jail, but in India evidently they can. I mean, not something weird, but they just up and get married, at least according to this lady. Anyway, she's really interesting, Trish. She wore a gorgeous sari too."

"We wondered if the principal was going to give her detention for breaking the no-midriff-showing rule," Gabi laughed, "but they just led her around like she was some cool lady."

"She wore sandals too, even though it was freezing the day she came to school." Maggie slowed down and started chomping on her handful of gingersnaps. Abe wished he had left Maggie back in the bike shed, but nobody seemed too concerned. Sara had started talking about a group of kids from East Lake who were at Model United Nations representing India, and all the girls wore saris for one session. Eis and Trevor had found some sticks and were playing cookie hockey on a flat spot on the rock.

So what was Maggie trying to say, Abe wondered. That incest could be okay, depending on the situation? And who it was? What kind of situation made it okay, Maggie? If it was fun? If you liked it? Was that enough to make it okay?

"Hey, Abe, get off your butt! I need a goalie on my hockey team. Trevor's shooting all my good gingersnaps into the creek!" called Eis. Abe jumped to his feet.

15

"It's Maggie's turn to baby-sit tonight, Abe," his mom said as she walked out the door behind his dad. We'll be somewhere for dinner and then at the Cameo for the movie. Burritos are in the freezer, okay?"

"You guys'll be back by 10:30 or so?"

"We'll be back."

"So shall I try that reply sometime when I go out?"

"We'll be back shortly after the movie and some coffee, Abe."

"Is it an R rated movie?"

"Abe, Dad's waiting in the car."

"Okay, Mom, have fun. But is it?"

"I'm sure it's a good movie."

The babysitting deal was a carry-over joke from about three years back when Maggie rebelled one night at Abe getting paid to "childcare" her. Having him in charge of her was bad enough, but to have him get paid for it drove Maggie crazy. So Mom agreed to give up childcare. But to make sure they were reasonable, she said, which meant they cleaned up the kitchen and didn't take all of Sunday morning to complain about how bad the other person had been, she took turns paying them $5.00 to "baby-sit" each other. They figured it was an easy five bucks, and whoever's turn it was also got to choose what video they rented.

"Bye, Mom and Dad," Abe could hear Maggie yelling out her bedroom window, and then to him, "You'll love the video I got, Abe."

He stepped down the hall to her bedroom door. "I better. You didn't even ask me what one I wanted. What is it?"

"A couple of Ramona movies."

"What?"

"You know, Ramona movies."

"Maggie, you are insane! We are not wasting a Saturday night on Ramona. They don't even rent Ramona movies."

"Yes they do. But that's not where I got them. They were at the library, and one of them I haven't even memorized."

"Maggie, we are not watching Ramona movies!" Abe remembered Ramona too well. Maggie and Gabi had memorized every Ramona movie the library had and turned them into plays which he had to sit and watch. He was serious about not doing Ramona.

"Did Mom know you got us Ramona movies?" Abe couldn't believe his Mom would walk out of the house so cheerily, probably headed for some great R rated movie, knowing he was home doomed to Ramona.

"Mom personally loves Beverly Cleary and her Ramona books. You know that, Abe." But Maggie could hardly finish the sentence before she burst out laughing and flopped back on her bed.

"Maggie, you dork!" Abe grabbed up her pillow and whopped her with it.

"Hey, no fair, Abe. Gimme my pillow."

He whacked her again. Maggie grabbed at the pillow, but Abe's hold was firm. Maggie sprang up, ran into Abe's room and lunged for his pillow. She had just clutched it when Abe whopped her behind. Maggie rolled over on the bed, doing a bicycle with her feet to fend off any more pillow blows, still laughing at Abe.

"Okay, Maggie, what's our real movie? And quit laughing or I'll..." and without waiting for the words, Abe's fingers hit Maggie's stomach in fast motion, then moved to her sides, and Maggie burst into giggles, choking over the words, "Stop, Abe. Tickling's no fair." He didn't stop just then. Maggie deserved it. She started the whole thing. He saw a bare spot of skin where Maggie's T-shirt had pulled up above her waist, and Abe reached for it.

But suddenly his fingers relaxed. Her skin was soft and warm. Abe let his hand slide just a bit instead of tickle. It was just a moment of hesitation, but in that moment the longing was overwhelming to let his fingers slide further up, all the way up under her shirt. To feel her, for real this time.

But Maggie sputtered out, "Quit tickling, Abe!" and she wiggled out of his reach and quickly rolled up and off the bed. Still laughing, Maggie grabbed up both pillows in her arms and ran for her room.

Abe swung his door shut and sat down on his bed, feeling shaky and hot. "Get out of here, Maggie," he said to the empty room, and fell backwards onto his bed. Abe looked up at Einstein. The poster blurred. His eyes were watery. "So, what's wrong with me?" he asked Einstein. "Did anything like this ever happen to you?" He stared at the words on the poster, something about wanting to know God's thoughts. "So, God, what's this all about?" Abe asked earnestly. He rolled over on his stomach and heard a light tapping at the door.

"What?" he yelled, realizing it was not exactly the voice he'd use if he thought it were God coming to answer his question. He knew it was Maggie, and the tone of voice was what she deserved. The door opened slightly and a hesitant smile appeared in the crack, along with the black case of a rental video.

"Treaty?" Maggie questioned.

"That depends on what that video is," Abe answered, and he quickly wiped his hand across his eyes. Maggie opened the door fully and said, "Tadah... it's your western, *Hallelujah George*. Mom said you told her it was one you wanted to get."

"It is," Abe sighed. "All this for nothing. Maggie you are insane."

"I know, Abe. Let's go make our burritos.

16

During lunch the next Friday Eis sat down at the table next to Abe. "Hey, man, I got my dad's pickup today. Wantta go shopping with me after school? We'll be done way before time for the game."

"Where to?"

"Safeway."

"You going grocery shopping?" Abe asked.

"Sort of. I got to buy a liver for Monday."

"A liver? Right! I love shopping for livers."

Abe wondered how Eis was going to pull off his Critical Mass presentation.

"I wouldn't have the guts to try it," Abe said.

"We'll ask if they have kidneys and gall bladders too, if it's guts you need," Eis quipped back. "But first priority is my liver."

Abe suspected Eis would change his mind over the weekend. It would be hard to make it work, especially if the kids in the class wouldn't be serious when they were supposed to. When he saw Eis get off the bus Monday morning carrying a cooler and a big bag, he knew the plan was on.

"The stage is yours, Mr. Eisenhower," Mr. R said, waving his hand grandly toward the front of the class. Eis put on a surgical gown and cap and a name tag, "Doctor Eisenhower." He pulled out a pair of Gandhi glasses from his pocket, switched with his own, and through the missing lenses, studied a clipboard chart.

He signaled to Phoebe, and she came up and put a pillow on the empty table in front of the class. She sat down on the table, swung her legs up, and lay down. The class laughed. It wasn't quite like Phoebe. She was definitely not the actress type. Abe had asked him why he wanted Phoebe for a partner and Eis had answered simply, "I need somebody nice." And then as if to explain, he added, "In real life it could even be a jerk, but for school I think it has to be somebody nice."

Eis spoke seriously to his Phoebe patient, "I don't have very good news, Miss Smith. We have not been able to find a donor."

"What are you going to do then, Doctor?" Phoebe asked softly.

"It's you who's going to do it. Keep hanging on a little longer. There's nothing else we can do."

"Doctor?" Phoebe began. "Could you change the visitation rules just today. I have some friends I need to say good-bye to... I mean... friends I haven't really talked to in a long time."

Eis turned to the class and said, "You've all come to see her? I didn't expect such a big crowd. But you can go in one at a time."

Then he stepped away from Phoebe a little and said in a quieter voice, "You must have understood that she's very ill. She needs the liver transplant today, or there won't be tomorrow. Oh, but she's waiting for you, to say goodbye. No, you don't have to leave your flowers back at the reception desk. Bring them to her as you come."

Abe didn't know about the flowers part. He looked to where Eis was pointing. Sara was standing with a big bunch of daffodils in her arms. Maybe a little faded, Abe wondered, like the ones the produce man at Safeway had in with the cart of lettuce leaves and old grapefruit.

"Go ahead," Dr. Eisenhower urged the students in the first row. "She's waiting."

Abe was pretty sure Eis must have prompted a couple of them before class, because they stood up, and then the whole row did, and they went back to Sara and got a flower. One by one they walked up to Phoebe, handed her a flower, and said "Good-bye." Abe was glad he sat in the back. At least he wouldn't be next. He was surprised when the next row, including Travis Brown, who Abe never saw do anything in class, all got up and went. And they were looking at Phoebe and not laughing like they could have been.

The third row got up and went to get their flowers, and then two of the guys nudged Lucas to go ahead and they stepped back. All eyes were on Lucas as he picked up a daffodil and slowly walked toward Phoebe. Lucas and Phoebe had been going together since the beginning of last summer, and everybody knew they really liked each other. Maybe it was Sara who turned on the music. Nobody turned to look. They were watching Lucas as the gentle words of the song filled the classroom:

The wondrousness of you
Fills my life with awe.
And makes me wonder when the world changed.
I guess I never knew
What it could be with you
And suddenly nothing is the same.
I love you girl.
You are my daffodil in spring.
I love you girl.
You are the warmth that summer brings.
I love you girl.
And when the leaves turn red and gold
And winter comes so cold,
Don't go away.
Please, always stay.
Forever is not long enough
For the wondrousness of you."

Lucas walked slowly to Phoebe's side, and then instead of handing her the flower as the others all had done, he broke the stem a few inches from the blossom and tucked the flower into her dark hair. He didn't say goodbye. He just let his hands fall into hers and stood there looking at her as if he was really feeling what it would be like. Abe felt his throat get tight. The room was silent.

Suddenly Eis broke out in a perfect Robin Williams genie voice, "I'll take that as a wish... and it is granted. The fresh liver squad is on its way!" Eis began wailing like a siren, and the two guys from the back, also now in surgery gowns and caps, with added booties, masks, and rubber gloves, rushed up to Phoebe carrying the cooler. They plunked it down on the table and flipped the lid open. Ice cubes fell out here and there, and the two of them simultaneously scooped out a big red-brown liver, and threw it onto the plastic sheet that Eis had just grabbed and draped over Phoebe. Phoebe groaned a little, then beamed.

Lucas had been pushed to the side by the rescue crew and started toward his desk when Eis caught up with him, grabbed his hand, and started shaking it wildly. "Now, don't you worry, Mr. Jensen. I'm sure we got that liver in time. Here, let me read the lab instructions." Eis rushed back to the cooler, pulled a card out of the ice cubes, and read it to the class: "Safeway guaranteed fresh hog's liver. Best if eaten by March 10th."

Abe doubted that Safeway would say it exactly that way, but it didn't matter. The class broke into laughter and Eis took a bow. Mr. R came from the back of the room and took Eis's hand. He didn't give it the wild kind of shake Eis had just given Lucas. It was slow and deliberate, and Mr. R said, "That was a powerful message, Mr. Eisenhower, and I thank you sincerely for your work."

17

When Abe's mom pulled up after practice, he was ready. He opened the back door and threw his backpack in, then got in the front. "It's not my great thing today, Mom," he said at the same moment she began her question. "It's Eis. You should have seen his presentation on giving away your organs if you crash or something."

"Pretty good?"

"If he would have had a sign up sheet, everybody in the class would have signed up their livers."

"So what did he do?"

"May sound kind of goofy, but he had us say goodbye to Phoebe, like she was dying because her liver had stopped working. And then he came in with this rescue crew and threw a pig liver on her lap."

"I see what you mean, Abe."

"No, really. It was great. Maybe you have to be there to get it. Like when Lucas went up."

"Maybe so."

They rode along quietly for a while, Abe thinking about Lucas saying goodbye to Phoebe and how his throat felt. He wondered if he should go into the Motor Vehicles office and get his license changed to show he was an organ donor. Maybe when it had to be renewed. And Eis had said he should tell his family. "So, Mom," Abe started at the same time she said, "So, Abe..." He let her go first.

Kathy Beckwith

"So how's your Critical Mass essay coming? Have you decided what you're going to do for a presentation?"

"Not really. I don't think I'll have to do mine till next week. I was thinking I just ought to get that friend of Grandpa Lewis's to come to school and talk about World War II. He must think war's pretty crazy if he was too scared to go to the beach for 50 years. Either that or I've been thinking about doing an art show. Get some army recruiting posters to put up." Abe stopped at that, purposely to get his Mom's reaction.

"Army recruiting posters? What's the angle?" she asked.

"I'd figure out a way to have them open up or have another display behind them or to the side that has all the real pictures of war from our old Newsweeks. I wouldn't have to talk, and I think they'd get the point." He paused, then added, "You got any good ideas?"

"Well, actually, I've been thinking more about what to have for supper than how to present war, but I'll think on it."

After dinner, Abe went into the computer room to do his math. It was hard to keep his mind on the problems he had to do. His head was full of other things. Abe reached for the phone to call Grandpa Lewis and ask if his friend might be willing to come to school. As he dialed he decided if the guy were too freaked to go to the beach he probably wouldn't be very good at talking either. He hung up before the number rang.

He wondered how Trish was coming on her presentation on incest. Abe had been embarrassed to ask her at school. Maggie would have, without batting an eye. Abe wondered if there was anything that Maggie would be embarrassed about. He smiled to himself when he realized there was one way he could find out. All he'd have to do was to pick out a Kayler Jordan video for some Saturday night and watch Maggie squirm. On second thought, maybe Maggie would like it. Maybe she would. That was a thought Abe let linger. He turned to the computer, and this time he knew exactly what he was doing.

He pulled up his old CRITMASS file and went to a clean screen. He had a few things he wanted to say about the movies. Abe wished the door weren't at his back, but he knew he could always hit the reset button if he had to. So he wrote what he wanted:

"I bet you'd like those movies Maggie. It makes you feel excited to watch that stuff. I could be on the camera crew taking the close-ups. No, I may as well be the guy doing it. He gits his hands all over her. And she starts reelly liking it. Next thing you know her blous is coming off. He's running his hands all over her tits. Nothing on them, just skin. Then he starts down her neck with his lips..."

Abe closed his eyes and felt his heart pounding. He went back over the scene a couple of times in his mind and let the arousal flood over him.

"I bet you'd like it, Maggie," he whispered. "Really like it."

When Abe opened his eyes the screen looked bright. And ugly. He slammed his thumb against the reset button.

"God, what's wrong with me? I came in here to do math." Abe whispered. "That's a prayer, Mom, in case you were going to say something about my language. Where are you anyway? Get this crap out of my head." Abe didn't know if he was talking to God or to his mom. He suddenly wondered why neither one of them had any clue how his insides gnawed, ached, how much he wanted this Maggie thing finished.

"One way or the other," Abe said out loud. He was shaking as he reached up to turn the computer off.

Abe went into his room and grabbed his basketball, but stopped and glanced up at the wall before he went out the door.

"Who are you looking at, so holy like?" he asked the Einstein poster. "Get out of here!"

Abe threw the ball against the backboard with such force that it rebounded out of the driveway and rolled into the street. He grabbed it up and dribbled it hard down the sidewalk. It was time to quit messing with this stuff in his head. Abe knew Maggie wanted it, as much as he did, or she'd cover herself up. She'd tell somebody about the shower. Girls like to have their tits felt. Anybody who watches the movies knows that. Maggie might be different than most people, but she was a girl with nice tits. Anybody would admit that. He had felt Maggie more times than he could remember— in his head. He'd even managed to rub his arm up against her when he pretended to escort her up the walkway. Maggie hadn't said anything, so she obviously didn't mind. He'd just give her a little surprise party. And she'd love it. Maybe she'd even want more than he planned, and he'd have to decide when they'd stop.

This Saturday night. With or without Kayler Jordan. When they were home by themselves.

Forget the prayer, God.

Kathy Beckwith

18

It was a crazy week for Abe, a week of pushing thoughts in and out of his head because he had to to survive. Sometimes everything seemed normal, so he pretended that it was. Sometimes he thought he was going crazy. Mostly he went through the routine of the day, knowing that something was coming and not knowing for sure if he wanted it or dreaded it. Just that it was coming.

Abe sat in first period on Friday, and realized that he had no idea what the Quotation for the Day had been. Mr. R was erasing it from the board and writing the names of the two groups that would present that day. Trish and Jenny were first.

Abe was surprised that Trish seemed nervous. She had been so confident, but he could tell a difference this morning. She didn't look at anybody very long when she talked, and she kept leafing through her papers as she did, like she was afraid she'd left something behind.

When Mr. R signaled that they could begin, Trish came to the front with a pile of books. Jenny carried a box and put it on the floor in front of them. Abe noticed the bold black letters on the box, H-A-T-S. Hats? he wondered. This was supposed to be on incest. But Trish had begun her explanation.

"I read a lot about incest, because I know someone who was hurt by it happening to her. I found out it's one of those things that a lot of people don't know what to do about or even how to talk about it. And so it keeps happening and more people keep getting hurt. I think it's like a lot of things. It becomes more important to you when somebody you know is affected. And if it's important, then you start to do something about it. What I decided to do is read you stories that tell you what people have gone through. Jenny and I will take turns. We're calling the name of our presentation 'Hats.' You'll see why."

They had borrowed two lab stools from the chemistry room. It reminded Abe of a Reader's Theater he'd gone to once. Jenny opened up one of the books, their U.S. History book, with a piece of paper stuck in it. She read from the paper. Her voice was soft and serious, not like the usual crossing-eyes Jenny.

"I got a cowboy hat for my birthday. I was 10. My dad said I looked like a real cowgirl, pretty fancy. He took me up into the hayloft and said he'd help me learn how to rope. He stuck one bale up on end among some other ones, so it wouldn't tip over, and he helped me practice till I actually roped it."

Trish whispered something to Jenny and she stopped reading, reached into the box, and took out a little red cowboy hat. She put it on and resumed reading.

"That was the first time he did anything. On my birthday. I've hated my birthdays ever since then, but for a couple years I couldn't let on. He said if I told anybody, they'd take me away, or my mom would leave us and we wouldn't have a family any more. He said he loved me and wanted to take care of me, and that this was a part of loving.

"Then I started going out with boys. It didn't seem to me that it made much difference what they did. I was already...used to it, I guess you'd say. My dad got so mad when he found out what I'd done. He called me a "slut." I just laughed at him, because by then I didn't care. I was a slut and I knew it, but he did it to me. Now I'm 16. I'm trying to get better, but I tell you, every time I see a red cowboy hat I get sick to my stomach."

With that Jenny took the hat off, dropped it down on the floor, and slowly and purposefully crushed it under her foot.

Trish opened a book, and then reached down into the box. Abe was surprised when she pulled out a wedding veil and clipped it in her hair. She began to read:

"I was trying on my wedding veil, but I started crying. I loved him so much. We'd been making our wedding plans. I looked at the veil in the mirror, but I couldn't look at my own eyes. I wasn't telling him the truth. He thought we were both virgins. Some people think that's no big deal, but it was for us. He thought that I had kept that gift of myself for him only. That was the way I had been with him and he expected I was the same with other guys I had dated. I felt scared. I didn't know what he'd say, or do, or decide, but I knew I needed to talk to him. I took off my veil and went to the phone."

Here Trish took the veil off and laid it on her lap. She continued reading:

"I asked him to come over, and when he came I said there was something he needed to know before we were married. I remember the look on his face when I said that. I told him I wasn't a virgin. He looked at me for a while and his eyes got watery. I put my head down. I couldn't look at his eyes. He was quiet, and then he lifted my chin and gently raised my face back up. 'That's in the past,' he whispered. 'We're here now. I love you.' I couldn't help but sob then. I loved him so much, and I felt so full of anger and disgust at the one who had stolen from me what was mine alone to give. And that thief would be at the wedding and watch me walk down the aisle and pretend that it had never happened. I hated his pretence. It ached inside me. And yet I couldn't tell. It was so long ago, and they would hate him. And I didn't want them to hate him. They wouldn't understand. I wanted to scream out, but I just cried silently."

Trish carefully folded the veil and put it back in the box. Abe looked around the room. Everybody was watching Trish and Jenny. Jenny pulled out the next hat, a baseball cap. A boy? Abe wondered. He knew that boys were sexually abused too, and he found himself curious about what Jenny would read.

"My name's Carrie," she started. A girl, Abe told himself. "I was fourteen." Like Maggie, he thought. "I walked home from softball practice as slow as I could." And here Jenny stopped and put on the blue cap. "I knew my brother Dan was the only one home. I hated being afraid of somebody you're supposed to love. It was crazy, all mixed up. I guess I loved him. But I didn't ever want him to touch me, ever. I didn't even want to talk to him.

"I had a funny feeling a couple of times that someone opened my bedroom door. It didn't have a lock, so I couldn't lock it or I would have, just so I didn't imagine things. I freaked about robbers maybe coming in the house and stuff, even though I knew it was crazy. And then one night, he was standing there, by my bed, my own brother, and he reached down and grabbed me, my chest, and said, `Where'd you get titties like that?' I was so scared, I didn't know what to do. I ran downstairs and wrapped up in the afghan, waiting for my dad to wake up. It was really early in the morning, but I didn't fall asleep. I just sat there all cold inside and out, but I felt safer downstairs. Dad was surprised to see me up so early, and I was scared to tell him, but I did. I think he was surprised too, and said he'd talk to Dan.

"It was later that day, Dan told me he was sorry, that our cousin told him that girls liked to have boys feel them. That one girl even took a boy's hand and put it under her t-shirt. I didn't say anything. What could I say? I just shook my head, like how could he listen to something like that. Or give an excuse for doing that to me.

"Then about a week later he came into my room again. I was asleep, but I woke up and he was leaning over my bed, touching me. I just stared at him and said, 'You get out of here!' and I ran past him downstairs again. When Dad got up I told him he had to stop him. He said he would, and Dan didn't do it again.

"But I still walked home slow from softball. I hated being afraid. I thought brothers were supposed to be part of your family. What a joke. A bad joke."

Abe felt sweaty. He hoped that was the last reading. But Trish held out her hand and took the baseball cap from Jenny. She twisted her long hair and flipped it up under the cap.

"I'm Carrie's brother, Dan," Trish said. "After that second time, my Dad kind of lost it. He wasn't just mad like he was the first time. He was scared, and he started crying. He didn't know what to do, but he told me we were getting help. I told him it was too late for help, that I was messed up and this was just a little part of it. I had never told him what happened to me at camp. I hadn't told him—or anybody—a lot of things. Dad called Aunt Leona and Uncle Ray to stay with Carrie and we went away for a two-day hike."

This is where Trish and Jenny started walking around the room, in and out of the rows of desks, so they were really close to us as they talked.

"We walked and talked for two days straight," she continued, "and we came home and told my aunt and uncle and some other people that we needed them to help me out of a mess." Jenny and Trish went back to their chairs in front of the classroom.

"There's no way you can feel how scared I was," Trish-Dan went on. "I knew everyone would hate me, even though Dad tried to tell me they wouldn't. I was in big trouble. I had touched a little girl I babysat for, and I knew that was against the law. Dad knew it too. I

Kathy Beckwith

wished to God that I would not have done that, but I did.

"Then something happened that I didn't expect. Dad asked me what I was going to do about it. I had only thought about how to keep it a secret for so long, that I hadn't thought about doing something about it. But when he said that, it was like for the first time in my life I thought I might somehow be okay."

Trish paused and then reached into the box and pulled out another hat. "No way," Abe thought. At that moment he wished he had half of Maggie's brashness. He'd raise his hand and interrupt Trish. He'd ask her what this Dan kid did to make things better? Did he end up in jail?

But Trish was putting the next hat on, one Abe knew well. Trish wore it a lot. It was a velvet beret, purple and black, suffragette colors, she had said one day. "Women's rights, in case you hadn't heard," she told them.

"This last reading," she said, "is short, and I think you'll like it. I'm wearing my hat because this is about people's rights and what can be done."

Abe watched as Trish picked up a book and turned to the back flap.

"I was a victim of sexual abuse as a child," she read from the book. "I tried to forget it, and I did pretty well sometimes. But only sometimes. And then the idea came to me that maybe it wasn't bad that I remembered these things. The memories have stirred me to write this book. I'm writing it for boys who have wondered if a 'crazy' thought is normal. I'm writing it for girls who just want to be safe. I'm writing it for young men and young women who want life to be normal even though the past hasn't been. I'm writing it for couples about to be married, or remarried, even though they'll think it has nothing to do with them. I'm writing it for you, because I want to share my belief that every person needs to live free from fear and hurt, and the family is the place where that begins.—Susan Wilson."

Trish closed the book and then turned toward the class. "That's the lady who wrote this book. The name of the book is *THE BOUNDARIES OF LOVE*. It's at the city library. Or rather will be when I check it back in. It's good, and you might not believe it, but it's even funny in some parts. My favorite part is a poem she included in the book called, 'If Little Girls Could Vote.' That's what gave me the idea of wearing my suffragette hat. I hope some of you will read the book."

Trish took off her hat and put it back in the box. She and Jenny started back for their desks, but then Trish stopped and said to the class, "No, what I really hope, why I did my Critical Mass essay on incest, is that if anyone in here even wonders if sexual abuse could happen to them, or that they could do it, that they'll get help." Trish's voice was shaky, and Abe was afraid she was going to cry.

"Just find somebody," she continued. Just talk to somebody." Trish took a big breath and blew it out again, before she continued. "And if there's nobody you can talk to, the book has a phone number you can call. I tried it to see if it works. They seemed pretty cool to me. Their number is easy. It's 1-800-GET-HELP." She sat down at her desk.

Abe noticed that her arm was shaking as she put her books down. He wanted to look at her, to see her face, to see if there were tears in her eyes. Instead he looked at the books. He saw the cover of the last book she had read from. It had big red letters and a white wall enclosing a bunch of hearts. He wondered what the little girl's poem was about, and what crazy thoughts boys might have that the lady wrote about. Talk to somebody, Trish had said. Sure! How could you talk to somebody about what was going on, when you didn't even know yourself? And who would listen? Not your folks. It wouldn't quite qualify as some "great thing you did today." The only person who ever listened was Einstein.

The thought came to Abe that he might just rip his Einstein poster down. He was getting tired of it. Besides, he had already decided what he was going to do. He didn't need Einstein's advice, or Trish's.

19

Everything slowed down after first period. Abe walked down the hall with the feeling that heat waves were rising in front of him. Things seemed hazy, and the voices around him were far away. Twice in math class the teacher asked if he was doing okay. The second time Abe answered that he was just a little sleepy, but he knew he was wide-awake. He was just in some other place where all he could see was the blue baseball cap that Jenny and Trish had worn, Dan's cap. He was glad there wasn't such a thing as a basketball cap. He wasn't anything like that kid.

Abe was the first one in the lunch line. He drank a few gulps of milk from the carton, wrapped his sub sandwich up in a napkin, and then took his tray back, dumping the carrots and celery. He didn't have time to eat them.

Trevor was in line as Abe headed for the door and said, "What? Is it crap today?"

"No, sandwiches. I just got to get some things done during lunch," Abe answered as he slipped past Trevor. Abe had decided to make a phone call. Not from the phone at the side of the main entry. He knew kids would be hanging around. There was another phone near the exit gates to the football field. He turned the corner of the building, and saw there was no one nearby. By the time he got to the booth his heart was pounding

Kathy Beckwith

hard and he felt sweaty. He set his sub sandwich down on the little counter under the phone and took the receiver off its hook.

"What am I doing?" Abe asked himself, and hung it back up, grabbed his sandwich and swung out of the booth. He peeled the napkin away from his sub and slid down onto the sidewalk, leaning against the chain link fence. "I'm okay. I don't need anybody," he said softly.

Abe bit into his sandwich and chewed slowly. He wondered if they could trace his call to this phone booth. His mom tried that once when some weirdo called the house, and they said they couldn't find the guy because he called from a phone booth. What would happen if they traced his call quick and set off the siren downtown? The seniors in the volunteer fire department would come piling out the front doors, run across the lawn to the parking lot, and hop in their cars for the fire station. Then in a couple of minutes they'd be swarming back all over the football field and the medical emergency van would be flashing its red lights and they'd run over to Abe and strap him down on a stretcher and haul him off to jail.

He used to do that a lot. Wonder what if. What if the glass walls on the West Tower in Seattle suddenly crumbled when he was at the top of it and threw him head first into the Matchbox car world far below. What if the steering wheel locked just when they were going around a corner and the car steered right into the path of a huge semi. Or if he'd play dead good enough if a bear started to chew on him.

But why would they want to trace the call? He was just going to find out if anybody would tell him anything that would make him change his mind about what he was going to do. He wouldn't say who he was or where he was from.

Abe wadded his napkin up and stuck it in his pocket. He went back to the phone booth. His hands weren't shaking like Trish's had been, but his throat felt dry. He cleared it twice and decided he'd better practice what he was going to say. It wouldn't be his usual "This is Abe Lewis and..." He'd say something like, "Could you tell me what you do and how you help people make decisions when they're thinking about something?" From there on he'd just have to see what happened. He repeated the sentence. It was too long. He knew he'd forget. He took out his billfold and found the sales slip for his basketball shoes. He wrote the sentence down on the back of it and then read it back. It sounded okay, so he slowly and calmly dialed 1-800-GIT-HELP.

The voice at the other end of the line answered on the first ring just as a puff of wind caught the sales slip. Whoever it was started talking while Abe was grabbing for the paper. It flustered him and he didn't really hear what the guy said.

"Northwest Hatchery and Supply. This is Jeff speaking. What can I do for you?"

"What did you say?"

"This is Jeff speaking. Can I help you?"

"Could you tell me what you do and how you help people make decisions when they're thinking about something."

"Well... Yah, I could do that. My main job is with the Araucana, Bardrock, and Bantams and I do office stuff and phones on Fridays and Saturdays."

Abe was confused. It sounded like some attorney's office, not a help line. But Jeff was still talking. "Does this decision you're talking about have anything to do with chicks?" Abe wished he wouldn't joke around. His mom had railed on him once when he called some girls "chicks," and he never had after that. Besides, Maggie wasn't a babe or a chick. She was just somebody who was there. And how was he going to talk about Maggie to somebody who made it sound like a joke? This Jeff guy had no idea how hard it was to call some place like this. The thought crossed Abe's mind that Trish must have gotten a different operator.

Jeff was asking again, "You calling about chicks?"

"No. Just one."

"One chick? Well, sure, we can do that. But if we're much of a drive, you might just want to stop in at your closest feed store. Most of them will be getting our chicks in in the next week or two. I know my first big bunch of Araucanas, Bardrocks, and Bantams are going out Monday."

"Feed store?"

"Sure. Where you from? I'll look up the closest one."

"Oh, no. That's okay. I'll call back later." Abe slapped the phone back into the hook. And then out loud, to the phone booth, he asked, "What? Who was that? Sure, Trish. Great crisis phone line. I think you got your numbers mixed up with some chicken place. Go to a feed store? Okay. When I need chickens. Right now I need something that makes a little sense. Abe turned around and walked slowly towards the building.

And then it came to him that here he was again, trying to fool himself into thinking he wanted to stop. The truth was, he knew he was in way too deep to get out now. He should have stopped this thing three years ago, when it was just porno, or at least before Maggie and her underwear started getting into the picture. It had gone way too far.

Abe felt rotten. He wished he were home, on his bed, where he could feel good. Einstein would understand.

20

The basketball team got out of last period fifteen minutes early to make sure they got on the bus on time. Abe was glad it was a Friday night away game at the school his folks rarely drove to. He hoped he got to play, but he didn't feel like having them or Maggie watch him tonight.

It was at West Grove, over on the coast, and they wouldn't get home until after midnight. He had plans to spend the night at Eis's. His folks wouldn't have to come get him late, and Eis's folks were going to the game and staying on at the coast for the weekend, so Eis was glad for the company. He had said they could use Saturday morning to go through a big pile of magazines in their garage for some more pictures for Abe's Critical Mass presentation. Abe felt relieved to be out of the house and away from Maggie for a while. He wanted some time to think, or maybe not to think. Tomorrow would come soon enough.

They got to Eis's about 1 a.m., and decided to watch a late movie. Eis brought mats and sleeping bags out into the living room and said they could sleep there. They switched channels around for a while, and found two old black and white movies, then one about a bank robbery in Atlanta. It looked boring. Abe didn't mind shutting it off.

He'd been thinking on the bus ride home. About Trish. Well, not really about Trish, but more about what she'd said in her presentation.

Abe wondered if Maggie would ever be afraid of him, if she'd want him out of the family, after he had felt her. This whole thing was supposed to be exciting, not scary, or at least not something that lasted if it was a little scary. Besides, Maggie wouldn't be afraid. She wasn't afraid of anything that Abe knew of.

He wished he had the guts to borrow that book from Trish, but he knew he'd never do that. He might find it at the library sometime and read it in the stacks, or at least the parts that might have something to do with him. But did it have anything to do with him? Abe wondered. He wasn't into incest. He was just going to play. And Maggie would like it. Or at least she'd let him do it. Besides, by the time he checked out the book, he'd know first hand what it would be like, and it would feel good, and he wouldn't need the book. He'd know by tomorrow night when his folks were gone.

They had to be gone. Abe knew it wouldn't be right to do it if they were in the house. Even if Maggie were quiet. It would be bad enough having Einstein there. But he'd do it in Maggie's room, and then even Einstein wouldn't have to know.

Abe had felt for a week that he didn't want anybody to talk him out of it. There was something exciting happening that made him feel good. All over his body. But now Trish was messing with the good feeling. He wished she had never given her report. Or if she had to, that she at least would have given them the right phone number for that help line. He wondered if they would have said anything about what would happen if Maggie told somebody. He wondered if they knew anybody who did it and was sorry. Kids his age. He wondered if they'd agree with that Carrie girl that Maggie might hate him. If it was somebody who would really talk, he'd ask them why it made a difference who you did it to and why girls had a right to let you see their stuff and then think nobody'd want to feel it too. He'd ask them how you stopped yourself doing something that you wanted and hated at the same time. Or not at the same time. That was the problem. Especially when the wanting started getting stronger than the hating. But they had talked about chickens instead.

On the bus ride home Abe's head had been filled with something too heavy for his neck to hold up. He leaned against the window and closed his eyes, but he couldn't close out his thoughts. He kept hearing Trish say, "Just find somebody. Just talk to somebody." She didn't know that he had tried and it didn't work. And he was tired of talking to an Einstein and a God that wouldn't talk to him. The only other person he could think of was Eis.

Abe didn't really like the idea of talking about something like this to Eis, but then he started thinking of every person he knew in the world. He only came up with two he would even think of talking to, Mr. R and Eis, and he didn't know where Mr. R lived. If Eis were being normal, he'd probably just make a joke about it.

He wouldn't have to know everything. If Trish were right, then maybe Eis would have an idea. Abe decided that anything would be better than the feeling he had now. He even asked God if there was any chance he wanted to kick into action and help out here. Then sitting in the dark bus on the way home from West Grove, he had decided to talk to Eis.

But Abe didn't feel so sure about talking now that Eis was really in the room with him and the TV was off and he had the chance.

He munched some of the chips Eis put out while he tried his voice out in his mind. It sounded calm and cool as it echoed off the inside of his head, kind of off-the-cuff sounding, as if the idea had popped into his mind for the first time just then. Abe waited till Eis shut the lights off. It somehow seemed easier to think and talk in the dark.

"Hey, Eis."

"Yah, Man. You okay?"

Abe realized he had lost the echo effect and was sounding a little squeaky. He told himself to stay cool. "I was just wondering about girls."

"What about 'em?"

"You ever get involved with one, for real?"

"Nope. But I have great dreams. And probably next week I'll invite Sara to run away with me and she'll say, 'Sure!' and then I'll definitely get involved. To the max, baby!"

"Come on, Eis. I mean in real life. Do you ever think about doing anything with Sara."

Kathy Beckwith

"Yup."

"Why don't you?"

"Don't want to."

"Don't want to?"

"Well, not before lunch tomorrow anyway."

"She likes you, man."

"Well, Abe, tell you what. You say that Good bread, Good meat prayer that Sara will come attack me tonight. I'll deal with the situation as best I can. Why you askin'? You planning something with Trish?"

"No way. I just keep thinking about things."

Abe decided to go on. Eis hadn't shut him down. "I keep thinking about shapes."

"I know what you mean, man. Round curves are a deeelight to the eye. We'll get to it someday."

"Eis...?"

"Yah..."

Abe swallowed hard, and then the words tumbled out before he could try to stop them. "Eis, if someone wanted to do something with a girl and he thought she might let him, maybe not everything, but maybe feel her and stuff, and see how excited she gets, and then see what happens, but he wasn't sure..."

"Hey, Abe, you're serious about this, aren't you?"

"I just keep looking at her and wishing I could put my hands under her blouse. Man, remember that movie we saw where that guy, Ladd, the hockey player..."

"I remember..."

"I see myself starting at her shoulders and running my hands down her arms to her waist and turning right around the front and coming back up to her..." and then he finished, "breasts."

Eis whistled. "Do I ever remember that movie and that move. That's not all he did, man."

"I know. I think about that too."

"And what does Trish say about all this?"

"Trish?"

"Yah, man. You don't just jump on somebody. You at least talk to her about your big plans.... so maybe they become her big plans, and you're both ready for it. That's not a gingersnap decision, Abe. It's big time."

"It's not Trish I think about, Eis," Abe said quietly.

"Why, you two-timing... Who are you dreaming about, man?"

"Maggie."

"Maggie? Maggie?!"

21

"Damn you, Abe Lewis!" Eis leapt toward Abe, grabbed him from behind and jerked his arm around into a piercing lock, forcing him face down onto the mat. "Don't you lay a hand on Maggie! She's your sister, man!"

His voice went wild as he continued, "You don't even know what you're talking about! You wantta end up in some shrink group, your family ripped apart, crying like an idiot because your sister hates your guts? Is that what you want? You want Maggie to hate your guts for the rest of your life? Shit! You don't touch Maggie, Abe Lewis!"

Eis sprang back, pushing Abe onto his side as he rose. "Who are you, anyway? You lay a hand on Maggie and I'll kick your butt so bad you'll hurt, man. You'll hurt bad." Eis lunged forward, dropped to his knees, and grabbed the front of Abe's T-shirt in both hands. He yanked Abe up to his face so that he was looking straight into his eyes. He finished in a low, angry voice, "And I'll do it, too. You better damn well believe I'll do it."

The light from the hallway shone on Eis's face, and Abe was surprised to see tears streaming down his cheeks. Eis threw Abe backward onto the mat. Abe didn't sit up but grabbed his pillow as if it could be some shield for what was to come next. Eis stood and walked over to the picture window, his back to Abe. Finally he turned to the couch and sat down. The room was silent.

Abe didn't feel anything. He wasn't scared, he wasn't embarrassed, he wasn't sorry. He was just empty and surprised. Surprised that his arm hurt. Surprised that Eis had blown up. That Eis had cried instead of making a joke. Abe heard the refrigerator motor kick on in the kitchen. Everything else was quiet.

Abe didn't like the idea of going home. It was too late, and he'd have to come up with some reason why he didn't spend the night at Eis's. But he knew he had no choice.

"Can you give me a ride home, Eis?

"No," Eis said matter-of-factly. "I won't give you a ride home. You're staying right here, and you're telling me what this shit is all about."

Abe didn't reply.

Eis stood up, and the next thing Abe knew he had bounded up onto a footstool in front of the couch. Eis spoke in some megaphone announcer's voice and said, "Attention please. May I have your attention, ladies and gentlemen? A reward is hereby offered for information leading to the arrest and conviction of whoever stole the body of my friend, Abe Lewis, scooped out his brains, and turned him loose on the streets to wander into my house and put on some idiotic one man horror show. Attention please. The amount of the reward will total exactly two million dollars and thirteen cents."

"Eis..." Abe didn't know what he was going to say, but Eis interrupted him anyway.

"Not so fast, young man. Everybody thinks these rewards are easy money. Read the fine print. It says 'for the arrest and conviction of.' Not just gossip. Not just, 'I think I might know something.' I'm here for the real stuff. You got some information worth two million dollars? Then start talking."

"And thirteen cents," Abe added. But that was all he could think of to say.

Eis stepped off the footstool and went over to his mat and sat down. "Abe, what's going on?" he asked. "For real."

That was the question Abe had wanted his mom to ask a long time ago. Or Mr. R. It was what he couldn't figure out, even with Einstein and God. He was glad somebody was finally asking it. He was ready to listen to himself answer.

"I don't know, Eis. I don't know. It's been coming for weeks, months, maybe longer. I don't know where from. It's just there, and I didn't know how to stop it. And then I didn't really want to stop it."

Neither of them said anything for a while, and then Abe took a deep breath and continued, "It was almost a mistake at first, Maggie being in the picture. I was just having fun with myself. And then she just got there. And it was still fun. At least while I was doing it."

Abe wondered if Eis would get mad again. He stopped talking.

"Go on," Eis said. "I'm still listening."

"I'd see her going from the shower to her room. Sometimes I wondered if she could see through the bathroom walls and tried to come out just when I was there. Because it happened a lot. She always put a towel around her but it was too loose and I saw her breasts. It sounds dumb, I know, but I kept thinking about what they looked like. And then the movies got all mixed in with it, that guy with his hands all over the girl's breasts and liking it, and one day Maggie was in my mind. I started imagining the scenes happening a little bit with Maggie. And then a lot with Maggie. I guess because she slept in the next room."

"Hey, man," Eis said. "You're not making sense. My dog sleeps in the garage. So?"

"I didn't say I was making sense."

"Okay. Keep going."

"Don't get mad at me."

"I already am. So, talk."

"I've had some magazines for a long time."

"Magazines?"

"Yeah."

"Crap! God, Lewis, you are so two-faced! I can't believe you! You didn't say a thing about porno when I told you how my mom blew up. And what was all that stuff in health class? I thought we voted it was cheap thrills and a sicko way to look at women."

"We never voted."

"You know what I mean."

"A lot of guys have that stuff."

"So what?" Eis shook his head. "We're talking about you...and Maggie."

"Well, I started getting these thoughts, I don't know, like maybe Maggie wouldn't stop me. That maybe she'd want me to do it. That maybe we could just keep it a secret. Or I could make her keep it a secret."

"You are a liar, Abe Lewis. You know good and well that Maggie wouldn't keep her mouth shut. And she sure as hell wouldn't want you feeling her up. 'And see what else happens,' you said. God, Lewis, you're a sicko. Like you could rape Maggie or something!"

"I didn't say I'd rape her. I just said maybe she'd like me to feel her a little. Hey, we don't have to talk about this. Just give me a ride home!"

"You're not going anywhere, Lewis. You've filled yourself up with some kind of crap that you know isn't true. What's wrong with you?"

"I don't know, man. That's what I'm trying to tell you. I don't know. Just give me a ride home. I shouldn't have said anything."

"Yah, you should have. I'm just a little bummed, that's all. You'd be bummed too if I told you I was really a hyena in disguise, and I had rabies. That's what this is like, man." Eis paused, and then he added, "It's way weird, but I think you better keep talking."

"I don't even know what to say. It sounds crazy to me too. I don't know, Eis. Don't you ever think dumb things when you're working away at it?"

"Of course I do. Dumb and great. Yah, dumb. But it's not hurting anybody, man. Don't you see the difference?

What you're talking about is trashing Maggie, a real person, your sister... and your mom and dad... and you. That's a whole lot different than dreaming up stuff.

"You may be smart in math and basketball, Lewis, but you're making an ass out of yourself when it comes to sex."

Abe didn't respond. Eis continued, "You want to know what really happens? I'll tell you. We talk about this stuff in my shrink group.

"One of the guys... I'm not supposed to tell stuff, but you need to know. It hasn't been much fun for him. His family's really messed up over the whole thing. He did it to his sister. 'Cause she wanted it.' He says he keeps remembering the look on her face. Said he never saw his folks hurt so bad. He told us what happened when his mom found out. She looked at him and said, 'How could you!?' The kid said he didn't even try to answer, because his mom started crying and saying over and over again, 'How could you? God, how could you do that? How could you do that?'

"The kid bawled when he told us about it, said he wished he was dead. He's in a foster home now. One without any girls in the family. Can't be around girls or kids anywhere unless it's in a class at school. He couldn't even go on a field trip without some special hotshot permission approval, which he didn't get.

Abe looked at the TV set. It would have been better to watch the robbery movie. He shouldn't have said anything to Eis.

Kathy Beckwith

But Eis continued, "Another guy was in some lock-up place for a while. I don't know exactly what happened, but it was with his stepsister and some other little girls. People get in big trouble just for touching somebody in the wrong place, Lewis. And what you're talking about is the wrong place!

"This isn't the movies, man. This is for real. Didn't you guys talk about mandatory sentencing in your State Government class? They can say we're adults and throw us in jail. For years. How would that feel, walking up to jail? They lock you up. They lock you up. You don't get out to go skim boarding at the beach. It's jail, Lewis. Sheesh. That kid has to register as a sex offender every year for the rest of his life. You'd like that? It's not quite the same as being known as a basketball star, or even a bad speller. You check in as a sex offender, and if you don't register, it's a felony. I think you better come listen to a few true situations, man, and learn the rest of the story."

Eis was quiet for a few moments, then he continued, "Maybe they don't put articles on sex offender registration in the porno magazines. Or about kids who are in debt for years even after they get a job, because they have to pay off their victim's counseling bill.

"And that's not even thinking about Maggie. What are you going to say to Maggie for the rest of her life? And to her husband when you meet him and he says, 'So you're the shit that molested my wife!' There's something wrong with the picture, Lewis.

"I'm just glad I go to my shrink because my dad used to beat me up so much. I'd never choose this kind of crap."

"I didn't choose it, man. It just happened."

"That's crap too. You have a brain. You can get help."

"Maybe that's what I'm doing."

"Okay. Okay, Lewis. That's cool."

And then Abe asked, "Your dad beats you up?"

"My other dad. When I was little."

They were quiet, both of them, until Eis continued, "Hey, Abe, I'm not saying you're crazy for thinking some things. I mean, I don't know, but I think everybody notices babes. Maggie is pretty, man. You should notice. Especially if she was just your little sister and then she's suddenly grown up. But you don't keep on it, man. You get out of the fantasy world. Whatever it takes, you get this shit out of your head."

"How?"

"I didn't say I knew how. I just said you gotta do it. You go play basketball or go running, or we watch cartoons instead of those movies we've been seeing. And you dump the porno right now. I mean every last thing, you throw it in the garbage. And you don't buy any more. You tell Maggie to leave the bathroom with her clothes on from now on, or something. Maybe you call those people Trish talked about at the end of her report."

"They're chicken farmers now."

"What?"

"They raise chickens and sell them to feed stores."

"What are you talking about?"

"I already called the GIT-HELP number. I got some chicken people."

"When?"

"Today. At lunch."

"Huh-uh."

"Yah. I did. Maybe Trish's book was old and they recycled the phone number again. All I know is I called them and this guy told me he sells chicks to feed stores."

Eis laughed. "Hey, let's try it!" He stepped into the kitchen hall and reached for the wall phone. "So, what's the number?"

"1-800-G-I-T-H-E-L-P."

"G-I-T? You called G-I-T?"

"Sure. Trish said it was easy to remember: GIT-HELP."

"Lewis, first graders learn how to spell 'get'! It's an E, man. G-E-T, get."

"Nobody says 'get'. It's git." But he had to laugh along with Eis.

Eis dialed 1-800-GIT-HELP, and repeated to Abe what he heard: "This is Northwest Hatchery and Supply. People hours are 8 to 6 weekdays and 8 to 8 Saturdays, closed on Sundays. Please call back. It's just us chickens here now." And Eis started some crazy bocking sounds.

Abe laughed.

"No, really. They have this chicken recording clucking their heads off. Listen." Eis held the phone out for Abe, but Abe said, "No, that's okay," and Eis hung up.

"So you got chickens. So you try again." Eis starting dialing another number.

"What are you doing, man?" Abe reached over and clicked down the holder. "You calling the real place? What are you going to say?"

"I don't know. Doesn't matter. I'll say whatever they have to know to tell me what to do to get your brains back."

"Not yet."

"Why not?"

"Don't tell them my name."

"Okay."

"Don't tell them your name."

"Okay."

Eis dialed the number. He listened to a message, then hung up the receiver and turned to Abe. "They said only the chickens are in right now."

"Right."

Eis laughed. "It was a recording," he explained. "They close shop at 12 p.m. Said we could call Monday morning at 6. And that if we need immediate help there's some emergency number we can call. Should we do it?"

"No. Not now."

"Monday?"

"Okay."

Abe suddenly realized that he was tired. He straightened up his mat and sleeping bag and lay down on top of it. Eis did the same. They didn't say anything for a long time, and then Abe unzipped his bag and crawled in. "What do you think they'll say, Eis?"

"I don't know."

"What if I get in trouble and they want to put me in jail or something?"

"They don't put you in jail for thinking weird."

"What if they say I've gone bonkers and I have to go to some counselor for the rest of my life and they tell Mom and Dad?"

"Well, you have gone bonkers. And the trouble you'd get into would be cotton candy compared to what could have happened. Besides, shrinks aren't that bad, really. Mine's a cool guy." Eis paused. "I don't know about your folks. They're pretty cool, but if I were them I'd be madder than snot."

"I don't want them to know."

Eis didn't answer.

"They think I'm good, mostly," Abe explained.

"That's lame."

"What?"

"Your folks think you're good, so you can't talk about bad stuff?"

"Stuff like war, yah, and drunk drivers killing people, but not if I ever got drunk or did something bad, or wanted to do something bad."

"I guess I never had that problem. We've all been bad ever since I knew us. But at least for some reason my mom decided we were going to talk. She has this theory: We're not bad. We just do bad things."

"What's the difference?"

"I don't know. Maybe you can quit doing bad things."

"They'd be ashamed of me," Abe said.

"So, we get them a shrink too." Then Eis laughed a little and said, "Hey, man, I got an idea."

Abe felt himself relax. He was ready for an idea that made Eis laugh. "What?"

"Let's you and me open our own shrink office at school. I mean, we got enough experience between the two of us, me being beat to a pulp for years, and you being an almost-reformed almost-sex offender and all. We could rope off one table in the cafeteria and set up a fast food/quick shrink consultation service and make that two million I almost lost.

"We're ready for anything. And if something new comes up we don't know about, I'll bring along a few extra gingersnaps they can eat till we figure out what to say."

"I thought shrinks just listened, Eis."

"Okay, so we'll eat gingersnaps while they figure out what to say to us."

"You're crazy."

"Then I'll be my first customer. I wonder what I'll talk about while I eat gingersnaps."

"How about your habit of jerking somebody's arm behind his back, half-way up to his neck, and screaming at the same time? My shoulder still feels that one."

Eis was suddenly serious. "Sorry, Abe. I haven't done something like that for over a year. That's the other part of why my mom and dad send me to the shrink." But then he added, "Hey man, you deserved it. I'd get you in a chicken-wing again in an instant."

"You won't have to, Eis."

"Well, just to make sure you don't go weird again, I'm playing super glue till this thing is settled. Maggie is going to think you suddenly grew a Siamese twin."

Abe started to say something, but Eis cut him off, "Whether you think you need me or not. And we call after basketball on Monday."

"Okay."

"I'll decide about your folks later."

"Who said you were in charge?"

"Me."

Abe knew he'd never tell his folks, but if Eis wanted to think he was in charge, Abe wasn't going to hassle him tonight. In a way he wished they knew. He wished they would yell at him for going to raunchy movies when he said he didn't. He wished they'd ask what Einstein sees from the wall above his bed when he's gettin' it on, what he pretends he does with Maggie then.

He wished his Dad would tell him what was normal and how you stay normal and what he did when he was sixteen. What he thought about girls and sisters back then. What he didn't think about them. How you get rid of Bell's Palsy when it starts getting you. He wished they'd go into his room and rip the magazines out from under his bed and throw gas on them and explode his whole room. Then the fire alarm would blare for real and Maggie would come running to his door with a towel around her and they'd all see what she does. They'd finally notice her nipples showing, and they'd yell at her too. Then they'd ask him what the hell was going on, except his mom wouldn't swear, but she'd feel like it. She'd get hot and sweaty, and Abe would start crying. And he'd cry, and his stomach would hurt. And his head would hurt, and his chest would hurt, and he'd cry and he'd barf. He'd barf all over.

"Yeow, Lewis! What the...." Eis jumped off his sleeping bag and yanked it away from Abe's.

Abe was crouched on his knees, vomiting into his sleeping bag.

"What's going on, Abe? You sick, man?"

"I don't know." Abe was shaking, gagging over his own vomit.

"Hey, don't do that, man, or I'll barf too. I never could stand the smell. You all right?"

"Yah."

"What was that all about? The 24 second flu?"

"I guess. Sorry about the sleeping bag, Eis. It's junked."

"I can see that. Go throw it in our washer. Only you have to pick the chunks out when it's done."

Abe rolled the sleeping bag up and started toward the Eisenhower's laundry room.

"You're not going to barf again, are you?"

"No. I'm okay."

Abe washed his mouth out and brushed his teeth while Eis got out an extra sleeping bag.

Everything was quiet for a long time, and Abe assumed Eis had fallen asleep. He ventured softly, "You awake?"

"Yah, man. I'm still awake."

Kathy Beckwith

"Think you could not tell anybody at school about all this. I mean, I kind of wish the whole thing had never happened. Even though it didn't."

"Okay, man. But we're both calling the non-chicken farmers on Monday after school."

"Okay."

The hall light shone on the sleeping bag lump that was Eis. "Thanks, man," Abe whispered softly. He felt light and calm for the first time in weeks, like maybe he was glad he barfed.

He thought about the call on Monday, and he knew he'd be scared, but he also knew he'd do it. Or at least Eis would. Abe was glad Eis hadn't given him a ride home. He was glad somebody besides Einstein knew what was going on. Maybe it could stop. Eis thought he was weird, but he was still willing to go into the shrink business with him.

"Yah, thanks, man," Abe whispered again.

Abe knew there was someone else he wanted to say thanks to. It was Trish. For doing her Hats presentation. He had a feeling that it was Trish who had started his stopping. He was glad she had the courage to do something that was hard, even if it meant your hands shook when you sat down. He was glad she had dumped the Ubvrdys. Whatever they were wasn't as important as Hats, at least not to him. He wished he wouldn't have been so hard on her. Maybe he could say that along with the thanks. But not tonight. Tonight he was tired.

22

Eis and Abe slept till almost 10:30 that morning. Then they went through boxes of old magazines for war pictures for Abe's Critical Mass presentation. That's when Eis said, "Lewis, you're doing the same thing the army does, so why are you belly-aching about them."

"What am I doing that the army does?"

"You said they use false advertising. Don't tell what they really do. Never put war pictures on the recruiting ad."

"They don't. They never do. So?"

"So neither do you."

"Eis, I'm not the army with some war going on or could go on that I don't bother to tell about."

"Oh yah?"

Eis and Abe pulled into the Lewis's driveway about noon, just as Maggie was coming out the back door headed for the bike shed.

"Hi, Eis. Hiya, Abe," Maggie called out. "Want to go for a bike ride? You could borrow Dad's bike, Eis."

"Not this time, Maggie. I gotta get home," Eis answered. Then he paused and added, "What if your dad needs it?"

"He won't. He hardly ever rides it. Besides, he's not home."

"What about your mom?"

"She has her own bike."

"No. I mean, is she home?"

"They both went grocery shopping. But Dad's bike is better than hers anyway."

Eis looked at Abe. "Yah, I'll stay."

Abe protested quietly, "Hey man, I'm okay. You don't have to hang around."

"You're right. But I'm going to." And to Maggie he said, "I'd love to go for a bike ride, Maggie."

"Abe?" she questioned.

Abe grabbed his sports bag out of the back of Eis's pickup and headed for the back porch door. Maggie persisted, "So? You up for a bike ride, Abe?"

"I just got home, Maggie."

"True," she said. "But not an answer to my question."

Yes, this was Maggie, Abe thought. He opened the back door and threw his bag into the corner. "Okay, I'll go."

Just then the Lewis's car pulled into the driveway. His mom opened the car door, and smiled.

"Perfect timing," she said. "Fourteen sacks of groceries, plus potatoes and milk, and three kids to unload them for us."

"Sorry, Mrs. Lewis," Eis said, "but I only work for gingersnaps."

"There just happens to be a two pound bag in one of those sacks, Eis, just in case you showed up this week, but I don't seem to recall which one it is. Guess you'll have to put all the groceries away too, so I can find your pay."

"On second thought, I think this is the week I carry groceries in for free, and come back later for gingersnaps." He reached for a couple of the sacks that Mr. Lewis took out of the trunk and headed for the house.

"Anybody hungry for a sandwich?" Abe's mom asked as she pulled a loaf of french bread from one of the bags.

"We were just ready to go for a bike ride when you guys pulled up," Maggie answered. "Can Eis use your bike, Dad?"

"He can use mine, Maggie," Abe said, "if he still wants to go. He doesn't have to now."

"Of course he doesn't have to, Abe. Dad doesn't care, do you, Dad?" Maggie asked.

"No, that's fine."

"We'll eat when you get back," Mrs. Lewis added.

"I mean, I don't really want to go on a bike ride anyway," Abe said. Then he paused and looked straight at Eis. "You guys go ahead." It wasn't what he had planned, but he knew what he was doing. And he knew that Eis knew too.

"Come on, Maggie," Eis said. We'll come back for gingersnaps and Abe after we get the bikes warmed up. Thanks for the bike, Mr. Lewis."

"Anytime, Eis."

Abe had been thinking about false advertising as he carried the grocery sacks inside. He didn't like the war going on and thought maybe, before he chickened out, he'd say something to his mom and dad. He waited until Eis and Maggie were out the back door, but only that long, for his Mom was already asking if he was sure he didn't want to go with them.

"I don't feel like a bike ride right now, Mom."

"Oh?"

"I barfed at Eis's last night." He hadn't meant to say that. But it was easier to say than "I want to talk to you guys about something."

She looked at him over her shoulder as she put the tuna in the cupboard. "Are you feeling okay now?" She turned back to the cupboard and rearranged some cans, "Or was it that long bus ride back from West Grove?"

She knew it was Maggie who got car sick, not him. She was just talking. So was he. And his Dad was putting the vegetables in the frig, not listening to either of them.

Abe wondered why he had thought he'd tell them. Maybe the army was smart to do false advertising. Who wants to know about wars anyway? You deal with wars when they come. If they come. And in the mean time you talk about shooting at a target and seeing the world and wearing clean camouflage. His folks didn't want to see him dirty.

"It was the bus ride. I'm fine now. In fact, I'm probably just a little hungry. I'm going to catch up with Eis and Maggie." He headed for the back door.

They were still at the bike shed. Eis looked surprised when he saw Abe. Abe shrugged and shook his head a bit, then pulled his bike out. Maggie just smiled. "I knew you'd come."

They rode as far as the Grange Hall before anyone said anything. Then Maggie said, "Speed up, slow pokes. Hey, I heard you beat West Grove, Abe. Were you the star of the game?"

"Sure, Maggie."

"He was, Maggie. He made nine points," Eis added. "And one basket was a three pointer that tied things up at the half."

"Hey, good, Abe."

Abe felt some of his anger at Maggie slip away.

"Wantta race, Abe? It's this thing we do, Eis," she added as she moved out ahead of them. "You can come too," she called over her shoulder.

"Thank you for not leaving me behind in the ditch," Eis answered.

Abe was surprised that they were at the Lost Valley turn off so soon, but he automatically sped up. "Sure, if you don't mind losing," he said, but Maggie was already ahead of him.

Abe pushed it as hard as he could, and gradually moved along side her. "Hey, Maggie," he called as he glanced sideways, but she was concentrating on the road and didn't even look his way.

"Sorry, Abe, can't talk."

"What is this, Maggie?" but he instinctively poured his strength into the pedals and left the question unanswered.

Abe knew he had never made that hill any faster. He too concentrated on the crest as he approached it, and as he felt himself being lifted up over the top, he let his feet glide and glanced sideways. There directly opposite him, almost in flight herself, was Maggie.

"Yes!" she screamed. "It's a tie!" Maggie sailed down the slope right alongside Abe. "It's a tie! It's a tie!" she screamed all the way down the hill.

"Now I can talk," she said, as they coasted to a stop on the flat where Abe used to wait for Maggie when she was little. Eis pulled in right behind them. "It was a tie, wasn't it, Abe?" Her whole face was one big grin.

"I doubt it. I was a nose ahead of you."

"You are a nose! What do you mean?!"

"You gotta be more scientific than just thinking it was a tie, Maggie."

"Eis, you saw it. Tell Abe it was a tie," she protested. "You know it was a tie, Abe, and you know your super scientist, Mr. Einstein himself, would agree with me!" Maggie said triumphantly.

Abe had to smile at her. "Okay, Maggie, it was a tie." And he felt pretty sure Maggie was right, on both counts. Einstein would approve. Of a lot of things. Abe was going to leave him on the wall and look him straight in the eye. "It's Saturday night," he'd tell him, "and the day is ending differently than I had planned."

"Wantta come over tonight, Eis," Abe asked. "Mom and Dad are going out, and Maggie and I stay home and watch Ramona movies."

"I would love to watch Ramona movies, Lewis." He paused, then added, "...if they are cartoons." He turned to Maggie. "Abe and I are turning over a new leaf, Maggie. The rules are... "

Abe kicked at his Dad's bike so hard Eis nearly lost his balance.

"Abe!" Maggie protested. "You almost knocked him over."

The humor of the moment before was gone. Abe stared at Eis. "What are you trying to say, man?"

"Nothin', Lewis. Nothin'. I was talking about cartoons. Ease off. You're the one who's kicking my bike over. You've got the problem. You're the one who's not talking to your folks."

"Shut up, Eis!"

"Sure, Lewis, whatever..." Eis whirled around on the bike and headed back up the hill.

"Why'd you kick him, Abe? Why'd you tell him to shut up?"

"None of your business, Maggie," he said as he swung onto his bike.

"Boy, this was a fun bike ride!" Maggie yelled out at them as they both moved up the hill.

Abe didn't try to gain on Eis. As he crested the hill, he paused and watched Eis stop down on the flat, throw his dad's bike down in the road beside him, and stand waving his arms out to the sides, blocking the roadway.

"What?" Abe asked as he coasted up, tipping his bike to rest one foot on the pavement before Eis.

"I happen to love you, man. I have no intention of doing anything to hurt you. At least not on purpose. I thought maybe you needed to know that."

Abe swung off his bike and reached for the hand Eis had extended toward him. As their hands met, Eis brushed Abe's gently away, reached for his shoulder, and pulled Abe to him.

"Don't give up on me," Abe whispered. His bike toppled to the pavement.

"No way," Eis answered. "I just thought you were hanging back to talk to your folks. They're cool dudes, man, and I think we could use a little help. I mean, so you're in remission now. What if you freak out again before Monday? Maybe I should tell Maggie what's going on so she could karate chop you or something. It's like this thing is too big for me, Abe. I thought you were normal, and now I'm starting to wonder if the whole world is messed up about sex. I already decided if the chicken help line doesn't tell us what to do on Monday, I'm calling my shrink."

Abe glanced behind him. Maggie was coming down the hill toward them. "Don't tell Maggie anything. I'm okay, Eis. I'm not going to do anything."

"Good grief. What is going on?" Maggie asked as she pulled to a stop alongside them.

"Nothing."

"Nothing? You two standing in the middle of the road hugging after you just yelled at each other, and your bikes crashed down all over the place? That's nothing? What if a car came over the hill? Besides, Dad hates it when people don't use his kickstand."

"I'll use the kickstand all the way back to your house, Maggie, I promise," Eis said, picking up the bike.

23

Abe stepped off the bus Monday morning and went directly to his locker. He needed a few minutes before first period started to figure out what he was going to do. The day was already a mess, and he didn't know if he could handle anything more. Maggie had left for school on her bike, yelling and crying. Abe had headed for the bus just because he had no excuse to do anything else. Maybe he should have just skipped. Gone somewhere. He didn't want to see Eis. The phone call didn't seem to make sense anymore.

"What's wrong with your sister?" Trevor's eyes searched Abe's as he approached the lockers.

"What do you mean?"

"She's in the office. The cops are there. I couldn't tell it was Maggie at first? Her face was in her hands and she was crying. Then they told us to clear the halls. Is it true what the kids are saying?"

"What!? What are they saying?"

Trevor paused.

"What are they saying, Trevor?" Abe demanded, but turned as if he couldn't wait for the response.

Trevor grabbed his arm. "I don't want to freak you, but a bunch of kids are talking about something that happened this morning. It's kind of mixed up. Somebody said a girl got hurt. Then I heard somebody say something about a rape. Not that it's Maggie, I mean, but just that something's going on."

"What are you talking about, Trevor!" Abe screamed as he pushed his hand away. He ran toward the office. He had to find Maggie, fast.

As he ran through the breezeway connecting the Science Wing to the rest of the school, Abe could see a big group of kids standing where the buses unload. He slowed when he saw a police uniform and several teachers in with the kids. Then he saw Eis throw his books down and break away from the crowd. He was yelling, and in the confusion Abe realized that Eis was coming toward him, with his fist shaking wildly in the air. A teacher was suddenly in motion too, running alongside Eis, moving him off the sidewalk, away from Abe.

Abe didn't glance back but ran on toward the office. He had to get to Maggie. The counselor, Ms. Olson, met him at the door.

"We have to talk with her, alone for now, Abe," Ms. Olson said. "We called your mom, and she said she'd get your dad and they'll be right here. Why don't you sit here until we've finished talking with Maggie? I need to be with her and the police officers for a few more minutes."

"Why?" Abe didn't have a chance to say more. Ms. Olson was gone. He didn't sit down. He realized that the chairs outside the office were lined up in a makeshift barrier, which he hadn't noticed as he ran up. Miss Carlson, the school secretary stood there, asking kids to go on to first period.

"I need to talk to Maggie, Miss Carlson," Abe said.

"They'll let you in in a minute, Abe," she answered. "I think they have to talk to Maggie alone first to get her testimony."

"Her testimony of what?" Abe said, choking back tears. "What happened?"

"Didn't anyone tell you?"

"No. Some kids said somebody got raped or hurt or something, and maybe it was Maggie."

"Oh, Abe, I'm sorry." Miss Carlson shook her head. "Maggie's okay. It was Gabi Garcia who was hurt. Maggie said they were riding their bikes to school, through Rabe Gulch, when a pickup hit Gabi. I guess it was several minutes before help came, and Maggie stayed with her. I'm not sure what happened, but it seems that the pickup just drove off, leaving them." Miss Carlson wiped away tears as she told Abe what she knew.

"Then Maggie's okay?"

"She's okay, but pretty shook up. We don't know how Gabi's doing, but I guess it was bad."

Abe slumped into one of the chairs Ms. Olson had pointed out. He dropped his head and didn't try to fight back the ache in his throat. Abe felt a hand slip around his shoulder and glanced up into Mr. R's face.

"You okay, guy?"

"Yeah," Abe answered softly. "And so is Maggie. Trevor said she was hurt." Abe knew his shoulders were shaking. He was glad for Mr. R's arm.

"I know, Abe. He asked me to come to the office and find you. Things were getting pretty mixed up for a while. Trevor said he gave you some bum information. It was what somebody told him. I guess "Rape Gulch" turned into about four different stories in a matter of seconds. Trevor knew you were scared."

The first period bell rang, but Mr. R didn't move. "I told Eis to start class, but I better get back. A lot of kids are upset. You okay?" he asked again.

"Yah, you can go, Mr. R."

But he turned back and said to Abe, "I think Eis wants to see you too. He said he thought somebody had hurt Maggie, and he was ready to cream him. He wanted you to know he's cool now."

"That was you, running with Eis?"

"Yes. I thought he was upset about the hit and run but he had heard the rumor of a rape too. I told him what I knew.

"What did he say?"

"Well, his exact words were `Good bread, good meat, good Lord, let's eat,' but he said it counts for a prayer, for Maggie and Gabi both. Then he asked if I'd come find you and see if you and Maggie were really okay. We're keeping everyone in first period until we learn more about what's happening. I'll check back with you later, Abe."

Ms. Olson stepped out of the office first. "Abe, Maggie would like you to come in."

Abe whirled up off the chair and stepped quickly into the office. Maggie stood up as he entered. Abe noticed a large dark stain on the leg of her jeans, but then his eyes moved to her face and he couldn't leave it. In that instant he wondered if that's what the boy in Eis's shrink group meant when he said he kept remembering the look on his sister's face. Maggie was hurt bad, Abe knew then, and then suddenly her face was buried in his shoulder.

"Abe. I needed you. They wouldn't let me go to the hospital with Gabi."

"I'm here," he answered softly.

"They wanted to take me to the Police Station. I said I had to go to school and find you. I had to find you. And then they made me stay in the office. Abe, it's all my fault. Gabi forgot her helmet," Maggie sobbed.

"I told her she had to use yours. But I didn't go get it." She pulled herself away from Abe's shoulder and looked at him with pained eyes. Shaking her head back and forth and biting her lip, Maggie continued. "I didn't get it, Abe. Mom was too mad at me for telling Gabi we could go when she didn't say so. You know how mad we were. I didn't want to listen to Mom, so I didn't go get your helmet.

"I said we'd share. I said she could use my helmet on the way home. Can you believe I did that? Her head was bleeding so much. I'm afraid she's going to die. Abe, please don't let her die. Please," Maggie sobbed.

Abe pulled her back to his shoulder and held her. Ms. Olson folded her arms around both of them.

"We'll be okay, Maggie," he said.

"Abe, can I talk to Maggie for a minute?" a voice gently asked. It was Tess, Zach's wife, from church. Trish was with her. Abe was glad to see them both, and didn't try to wipe away the tears he felt on his face, not knowing if they were Maggie's or his own. Abe noticed the police officers saying something to Ms. Olson, and then they slipped out of the office. Maggie turned to Tess and started sobbing again.

"Tess. I hurt Gabi. What can I do?" Maggie cried.

"You didn't hurt Gabi, Maggie," Tess answered. They told me you stayed with her until help came. The pickup hurt Gabi," she said.

"But Tess..." Maggie cried.

"Maggie." Abe turned her face towards his. "Sometimes things happen. Sometimes we realize later what we should have done. You didn't mean for Gabi to be hurt."

"I know, Abe. But maybe with a helmet she wouldn't die."

"When your folks come, Maggie," Tess said, "we'll go to the hospital."

"Can we pray for Gabi, Tess?" Maggie pleaded. "Can God please keep her alive?"

"Yes, Maggie, we'll pray," she answered.

Abe didn't hear exactly what Tess said there in the office, but they all held hands like they did at youth group, Ms. Olson too, and Abe silently said his own prayer, to God, "Thank you for keeping Maggie safe, God, from everything." And then he added, "And can you help Gabi? Please. Maggie thinks she's hurt bad, but I guess you know that."

The rest of the morning blurred by for Abe. He went with Maggie and Tess and his folks to the hospital. Gabi was in surgery when they arrived. Abe wondered if Mr. R had a quote for the day about how to keep somebody alive.

Gabi's parents were there too, and his mom and dad just hugged them, without saying anything, but they were all crying. He wondered if Gabi needed any organs and he thought maybe Eis would come to give her some, and then he realized that he wasn't thinking right, that it worked the other way, that Gabi would be giving up her organs if she died. He wondered if that would make her mom and dad feel any better, and he looked at them and knew it was Gabi they needed, not for somebody else to stay alive because of her liver.

Sometime after noon they went to the hospital cafeteria for some lunch. He and his dad took the first shift.

"How long do these operations take?" Abe asked his Dad.

"I don't know, Abe." His dad looked at him and lines formed across his forehead. He teeth were clinched. Abe wondered if he was going to cry. "Gabi is bad, Abe. I'm worried that it's not going right." He put his fist up to his mouth and tapped his teeth. "Do you realize we could have lost Maggie today?" Abe realized then that his Dad was crying, trying to hold it back. Still the words came out, "God knows how much I love you two kids." He lowered his fist and opened it over Abe's hand. "Don't ever forget that, Abe, no matter what."

Abe scooted his chair away from the table, bent over in it and sobbed quietly. For the pickup missing Maggie. For the look on Gabi's mom's face. For his dad's hand on his. For what didn't happen last Saturday night. For Trish believing in hot line numbers. For Tess coming to pray with them. For Eis offering a two million dollar reward. For Maggie letting Gabi bleed on her jeans. The thoughts were all mixed up, but his Dad's hand was still there, on his.

"Some day I've got to talk to you, Dad, about a lot of things."

"Okay, Abe. We will," he answered.

They ate a sandwich without saying anything, and then Maggie and Tess were there beside the table.

"Mom said maybe you could just bring them some coffee, Dad. They don't want to leave the waiting room."

"Okay, punkin," he answered softly, then took his tray to the conveyor belt and went to get the coffee.

"Can we join you, Abe?" Tess asked.

"Sure."

"They have turkey noodle soup, Maggie. If that's okay, I'll get two bowls," Tess said.

But Maggie hadn't even answered when they saw Mrs. Lewis standing in the doorway to the cafeteria. Her face was full of pain, and she motioned limply for her husband to come. Abe saw tears streaming down her cheeks.

"Abe?!" Maggie pleaded, and then she turned and ran.

24

Eis stood at the Lewis's back door. "They told us at school that Gabi died. That's so bad. Is Maggie okay?"

"I guess. She's in her room, crying. Mom and Dad are with her."

"I'm so sorry, man. That guy in the pickup oughtta rot in jail for the rest of his life."

"Who was it?"

"They still don't know. But they'll get him."

Neither of them said anything. Then Abe asked Eis in. "Want something to eat? Or some juice or something?"

"No thanks. I think I'll go on home. I just wanted to come see you guys." Eis turned to leave, and then looked back at Abe. "You know, I got Dad's pickup so we could call the hotline after basketball today. But they aren't even having practice. Kids are hanging around in the gym, sort of like they don't know what to do, but don't want to go home either. I don't know. It seems like a crazy time to call."

"We don't have to call anytime. Really. The whole thing was crazy. It's over. That's all. I could never hurt Maggie, Eis. I wouldn't do that."

But the Saturday after Gabi's funeral, Eis appeared at the back door again. "I been thinking, man. We still gotta call. I'm not going to spend my life wondering if, when everybody stops being sad, you're gunna go off your rocker again. Nobody's home at my house. We can call from there. Come on."

Abe left a note for his folks on the counter, and headed for Eis's pickup. He really intended to talk Eis out of calling altogether, but his reasons why it wasn't needed didn't seem to impress Eis. Finally Abe said, "I'm not going to do it, man. I'm okay. I don't need any help."

"Well, you weren't okay."

"I am now. And I'm not calling."

"Then I am."

Eis went straight to the phone and dialed.

"Hold on. Can we talk about this?" Abe reached up to disconnect the call, but Eis pushed his hand away.

"No way. Listen on the extension if you want. I'm calling."

Abe stepped into the living room and picked up the other phone as a voice answered, "Get Help Counselor. How may I help you?"

Abe mouthed, "No names!"

"May I help you?" the voice repeated.

"Sure," Eis said. "I have this friend who's gone crazy..."

Abe rolled his eyes, but Eis continued.

"He hasn't done anything yet, but a week ago he was about ready to attack his sister. Sex stuff."

Abe jerked his hand up in protest, but Eis didn't even pause.

"He's usually a normal guy, smart and nice, but we don't know what to do about this."

"So he knows that you're calling?" the counselor asked.

Eis laughed, "Yeah, he does, but he's chicken to talk himself."

"Is he with you?"

Abe shook his head furiously, and Eis answered, "No, not right now. He keeps saying he's okay, but I'm worried that maybe it could happen again, and somebody could get hurt."

"So your friend told you that he planned to sexually assault his sister, and you're worried that it could still happen?" she asked.

"Yeah," Eis confirmed.

"Well, first let me say that I know it took a lot of courage for you to call. You're right on. It's the right thing to do. If he told you about this, he's obviously reaching out for help, and it shouldn't be ignored. Please tell me more about what's happening with your friend."

"Well, nothing yet. It's just that it was almost ready to happen." Eis recounted for her the events of last Friday night and what Abe had told him. She asked some questions, and Abe found it all sounding so odd, hearing other people talk about what only he and Einstein had known for so long. She asked if the friend had talked to anybody else about this? Eis said he didn't think so. Abe confirmed by shaking his head.

"What about his parents?"

Abe mouthed, "No!" and Eis answered, "Not yet."

"Do you think he plans to?"

Abe shook his head as Eis said, "They're cool. But I don't think he wants to."

"Have you discussed other choices with him, what he might do now?" she asked.

Eis looked at Abe, but didn't wait for an answer. "His top choice is to do nothing and hope the problem is solved. But frankly, I'm worried, or at least I need somebody to tell me that I don't need to worry."

"No. You're right to be concerned," she replied. "One thing that might help your friend is to speak to someone besides you, an adult, he can trust and who may be able to help him. Does he have this hotline number?"

"Yeah, we got it at school," Eis answered.

"Good. We also need to think about his sister, and make sure that she is safe right now. We can't necessarily trust that we know the whole story."

Eis looked at Abe. Abe covered the receiver with his hand and said quietly, "I haven't touched Maggie."

Eis continued, "Well, I don't think he's done anything, and I think he thinks he won't hurt her. There's this sort of mess going on because a girl at our school got killed, and I don't think anybody's quite back to normal yet. But I guess what I'm wondering about is when we do get back to normal, how do I make sure he's back to normal too?"

"There are several things that can be done," she said. "What have you thought about?"

"I don't know. Maybe for him to go to our school counselor, or for both of us to go," Eis said. "But is he going to be okay if we wait till Monday?"

Abe flung his head back, and waved his arm in frustration at Eis.

"That's important to ask," she said, "and not always easy to answer. I'd want to know if the boy and his sister are alone in the house, and if she's aggressive in letting someone know when something is moving out of bounds. That can be surprisingly hard to do. Do you know the girl?"

"Well, I know Mrs. Lewis is sticking with Maggie a lot these days because of Gabi dying..."

At this point Abe threw the phone up into the air. "I can't believe you!"

It landed with a thud on the carpet, and Eis said, "Oh, sorry, I dropped the phone. My little brother just came in and is making too much noise." He motioned for Abe to be quiet, then continued, "I think we're okay. This guy's sister isn't shy at all, so I think she'd just tell him to knock it off, or she'd call for help, and like I said, her folks are home a lot right now."

"You suggested that he, or both of you, could talk to your school counselor. Can you really do that?"

"Sure. Ms. Olson would make the time. And we both know her."

"Eis!" Abe yelled.

"Oops," Eis said into the phone. "I said I wouldn't tell any names. At least not till we figure out what you're going to do. He's scared about getting in trouble."

"I don't need any names," the counselor said. "What I want to do is make sure you have the help you need. And the help your friend needs. Usually we don't learn about things like this until it's too late. It's good you called now…"

Eis stretched up tall, and with his free hand, reached over and patted his own back.

"…and I'm very glad your friend talked to you," she continued. "Most often perpetrators get locked into thinking they can't tell anyone what's going on in their heads. They're afraid to get help, and so they don't.

"I think your plan to check in with your school counselor is good. Remember that you can call and talk to us again if you want. And I'd like to give you another hotline number that will be open, even when we're closed. You or your friend may call them anytime, toll free, to talk about this."

Eis pointed to the pencil and notepad on the table in front of Abe. "Write it down," he mouthed. "With the right spelling," he said to Abe, then realized he had whispered that into the phone.

"Surely," the counselor continued. "It's 1-800-4-A-CHILD." She spelled c-h-i-l-d. Eis grinned at Abe, but he just rolled his eyes in response.

"Got it," Eis said.

"And I'd like to ask something else," she added. "Can you be with your friend, available to talk with him about this, until he gets to the counselor you mentioned."

"Totally," Eis said. I've already been doing that, at least when he's around Maggie." Eis glanced at Abe, and, seeing the look on his face, said, "Well, I better go. Thanks."

He turned to Abe. "Sorry, man. Sorry. It was just like I was talking to this lady who already knew us, and the names just slipped out. But I didn't say who you were, Perpetrator."

"Don't call me that."

"Okay."

"I'm the only son of a Mrs. Lewis who has a daughter named Maggie who has a friend named Gabi who just died and goes to a high school where Ms. Olson is the counselor. All she has to do is plug me into a computer and it prints out ABE LEWIS: Lock him up."

"Hey, relax, dude. Nobody's going to lock you up. And that lady is probably from New York somewhere. There are a million Lewis's in New York alone, and she has 49 other states to get to before she finds us. Besides, what's so bad if she knows? We're going to see Ms. Olson on Monday anyway."

Part IV. MAGGIE

I was thinking tonight about how fast you change what you think is important.

Three weeks ago on Saturday I would have told you that the most important thing in my whole life was that I finally beat my brother, Abe, in a bike race. Well, I didn't actually beat him. We tied. But I've been trying to tie him ever since I could ride a trike, so it felt like I won.

And now I don't ever want to see a bike again.

My friend, Gabi Garcia, died two days after that. From a bike wreck. She put her head on my leg and told me to stay with her. I wouldn't have left her, you have to know that, but I wanted to. I wanted to ride somewhere fast and call 9-1-1 and have the ambulance come and stop the bleeding from Gabi's head. You see, it was my fault she didn't wear a helmet.

I have to tell you one more thing, so you won't hate me, even though it doesn't really matter now to Gabi. The doctor said that she died because of a ruptured spleen and some other injuries in her stomach and chest. I'm so glad they don't make helmets for that. Oh, I didn't mean that, not like it sounded. What I meant was there should have been some kind of armor suit that could have kept Gabi totally safe. But at least I wasn't the one who didn't have her wear a stomach helmet. Which means I didn't really kill her. I know that doesn't make her come back alive, but I cried a lot after the doctor said that about her spleen. I stopped thinking about killing her, and started realizing I'd never see her again.

I couldn't believe that my precious friend Gabi was gone. That we couldn't ever ride bikes anymore. Or French braid each other's hair. Or do quotes from all our best movies, especially the funny ones. She is the best Diana and I do Anne of Green Gables, or rather we did.

You know how Gabi and I say goodbye? We twirl our thumbs at each other. I forgot to do that before they put her in the ambulance. I never told her goodbye. And now I never can.

The day after Gabi's funeral, my mom picked me some tulips from our yard. She put them in a vase and set them on the dresser in my room. I looked at them a lot for the next couple of days. Did you know they close up at night, and then the next morning they open up again, and then they close up again that night? They don't seem to realize they're already dead. They just keep on doing what they're supposed to do, and they're really dead the whole time.

I think that's what people wanted me to do. Open up and close up and open up and close up, and pretend I wasn't dead. But I was. Not like Gabi. But still I was.

I played the piano a lot that week. "El Shaddai," mostly. A couple of other songs that let you feel sad. I'm glad I knew them by heart because it would be hard to figure out the notes when your eyes are blurry. And then Mom said I had to go back to school. I didn't want to.

Kathy Beckwith

First period I have science. We were dissecting clams, trying to find their hearts. I wondered if they had spleens. I wondered if everybody was staring at me. But second period was English, and Ms. Dunlop said we were going to talk about what it's like to survive something awful. Just like that. Like I couldn't get out of it. And we did. And I cried. And some other kids cried. And I was glad I was back at school.

When I really knew maybe I wasn't a dead tulip after all, was about a week later. I sort of have this bad habit of forgetting to turn on the exhaust switch when I take a shower. It gets all steamy in the bathroom and then when I open the door, the steam goes right out to this smoke alarm that's in the hall between Abe's room and my room. Well, Abe hates it, because he tries to sleep too late, and it wakes him up. Or sometimes my dad's toast sets it off. Because the toaster didn't work right.

Anyway, the alarm went off, and I just went back into my room and flopped down on my bed and cried. I don't know why. I guess because I messed up again and Abe would be mad and I still missed Gabi. And then what happened is the important thing.

Abe came banging on my door, saying, "We gotta go, Maggie. We gotta get out of the house," even though he knew it wasn't a real fire. I couldn't believe it. That's what I say to him, and I got in trouble for it by Mom who said I'd better lay off for a while because I was making Abe so mad. So anyway, I couldn't help but laugh. I didn't think anything would ever be funny again, but I laughed, and so did Abe. But we didn't go outside, because all I had on was a towel.

That's something else I should mention. Not the towel, exactly, but a whole bunch of things related to it. It happened a few days later, after the fire alarm went off once more, from the toast. We had a family meeting, I guess you'd call it. It started out just to be breakfast, but then Abe came. He said he had three announcements, like he was in charge of the world or something.

First, we weren't keeping the toaster one more day. Second, he, Abe, and not Maggie, was in charge of his own fire drills. And third, Maggie, me, was not wearing her old nightshirt around the house anymore. I didn't see what that had to do with the toaster or fire drills, but Mom looked at Abe and then looked at me and said, "You do need a new night shirt, Maggie." And Dad got up, unplugged the toaster, and threw it in the garbage can.

That was just the beginning. Abe said he had to talk to Mom and Dad. He wasn't being bossy anymore. In fact, he was real quiet. Like something was wrong. For a minute I thought maybe he had cancer or something and nobody told me. But then I realized Dad and Mom didn't know about it either. They acted worried, because frankly, Abe never says "We gotta talk." So Dad called and said he'd be late for work that morning.

Abe told Mom I needed to go into my room, which I didn't agree with, but Mom said I had to. She said I should get ready for school, so I went, but I left my door open. I maybe should have tried not to listen, but I figured if Dad was going to be late for work so he could hear what Abe said, then I should hear too.

It wasn't easy from my room. Finally I decided just to come out, but by then Mom was on the porch waving the bus on, like we were taking her car to school that day. That's when I realized this was big stuff. So I just sat down on the floor next to the couch. Abe started to object, but Dad said maybe I should be there. We talked for three hours.

I don't really want to say what it was all about. It's embarrassing.

No. I'm going to tell you exactly what it was about. Because that's the whole thing that made it a problem in the first place. Keeping things a secret that I guess we should have talked about the very first time they came up.

You will think this is really weird. And maybe I don't want you to know. I want you to like Abe. Because he really is nice. And I'm afraid if I just tell you what happened, you'll think he's a jerk. Well, he's not, so here goes.

Abe has been going berserk recently. Or maybe for longer than recently.

Yuck. I can't do it. I'll just tell you what I learned.

Number 1. You can't always tell about brothers by the way they act. Sometimes they have a lot more going on in their heads than you think. Well actually, I only have one brother, who you know is Abe, so I can't say for sure about all brothers, but at least in one case, normal brothers can be weird.

Number 2. Bodies are funny. I mean who would think they could cause so much trouble. I'm sorry if that doesn't make sense, but that's all I can tell you, for now. Except that I did get a new nightshirt, a Minnie Mouse one. And Mom got a new toaster too, but that's not really about Number 2.

I guess I could say a little bit more. Some of it comes from quite a while back, but it ties in.

Abe and I share the same bathroom. Mom and Dad have one in their bedroom, so they never use ours. I guess it used to have a lock on it when I was little, but Mom said I was always locking myself in, or locking the door and closing it behind me on purpose, so they changed the doorknob to a non-lock kind. They said we could just knock to find out if anyone was in the bathroom.

Well, that was a bad idea. I don't think it was any problem until a couple years ago. Then Abe started getting mad at me for taking so long in the shower, and a couple of times he just stuck his head in the door and yelled at me to get out. I yelled back that I'd get out when I was ready and he wasn't my boss. Then he came into the bathroom and yelled at me to hurry up, and once he stayed there and brushed his teeth while I was in the shower. I didn't know what to do. I yelled for Mom, but I don't know where she was because she never answered. I never told anybody that Abe did that. Then one time he slid the shower curtain open and reached in and turned the cold water on full blast.

I still didn't tell anybody. I'm not actually sure why. Maybe I thought I'd get in trouble for not telling before,

Kathy Beckwith

when he first put his head in the door or when he came in, like I was in on it, or it was my fault for letting him brush his teeth in there. Anyway, I didn't like it, but when I didn't say anything when it first happened, it just seemed like I couldn't tell about it later. I tried to forget it. I tried to pretend he probably didn't even see me.

But I guess it mattered to Abe. He said he thought maybe I didn't care. I did. He thought maybe I wouldn't tell. Which I can see now why he thought that, because I didn't tell. But you can bet I'll scream my head off if he ever touches the bathroom doorknob again, when I'm in there. But we got a lock on the door, so that won't be a problem.

Anyway, he also thought it was bad the way I wore the towel back to my room. I honestly didn't think I was being bad. I thought I was covered up. But anyway, I guess it mattered to Abe, along with some other things. Dad asked him what other things.

Abe confessed about these awful sex magazines and raunchy movies he'd been going to when he said he wasn't. Anyway, it got pretty bad, but Dad kept his cool and said he thought maybe it was a good thing Abe had called the meeting. That it was high time we sorted some things out. I actually thought Dad might rail on Abe some, because it was really off the wall, but he didn't. So I did. I asked Abe didn't he pay any attention in youth group when we had the lessons on pornography. I said, "Gol, here Mom and I are protesting the posters in Charlie's Market because they are using women's bodies to sell beer, and here you are hiding them under your bed!"

He just looked at me and said, real soft, "I was wrong, Maggie. I am so sorry." So I didn't say anything more. That's the side of Abe I hope you see besides the junk.

He apologized to Mom and Dad too. He said he didn't feel like a very good person. He wanted to stop it all so many times, but he just couldn't. He couldn't tell anybody because they thought he was good. Like they knew he wouldn't do porno or lie about junk movies and he had already done both, a lot.

He said, and here I know you'll barf because it's definitely barf material, but he said he had some of my underwear in his room. Mom covered her face with her hands then and started crying. I guess because she thought Abe was a sicko. At least that's what I thought! How could she not know what was happening for all these months, she sobbed. What went wrong? How could she not have been there for Abe? Thank God somehow this got stopped.

That's when Dad stood up and said, "Hold on." He walked over to the frig and got a bag of blueberries out of the freezer. He told everybody to eat fifteen of them before we said one more word. So we did. They're really good. Better than Popsicles, kind of creamy instead of icy.

Abe told us he had talked about it to this friend of ours, Eis, and they were going to tell Ms. Olson at school when she got back from some conference.

At the end Dad said that his insurance gives us all some free counseling, so he and Mom decided this would be a good time to use it, with Gabi dying and all, and then this stuff with Abe.

So that means I am officially a psycho-case, which I think is kind of cool, because ever since grade school I loved the counselor because she had all these great posters on her walls and boxes of puppets and the best toys. But I never got to go to her office. I only looked in at the door. Abe said that we weren't going back to grade school and if all I wanted to do was play with puppets then I was insane

I also learned a Number 3. This is it: It's pretty cool to have a brother who isn't afraid to cry. I guess I knew he cried when he was little, but that doesn't count. Or when Gabi died, because I didn't really notice then. To know he would cry because he wanted to be friends with me when I was an old lady is something else.

I cried too, if that makes any sense. It probably doesn't. Maybe I am a little insane, but I think Abe's as insane as I am. I know for a fact that he talks to the Einstein poster in his bedroom.

When he got his first English grade this year, which happened to be an A, I heard him ask Einstein if he ever got an A in English. I poked my head into his room and told Abe it wasn't a fair question, that he should ask Einstein if he ever got an A in German. You see why, don't you? Because he was born in Germany. Anyway, you can probably guess what Abe said.

Sometimes I still think Abe is a little insane because of our family meeting, but I'm not worrying about it tonight. I guess some things just don't make sense. Like why Abe would think some things. Like why that pickup came so fast behind Gabi right at the narrowest place in the road. With Gabi, help finally came, but it didn't do any good. With Abe, he says it got there just before the crash. I wish with all my heart that could have happened with Gabi. Then everything would be okay.

—Maggie

THE END

Kathy Beckwith

Author's Postscript:

A group of teens who read this book when it was still in manuscript form asked me to explain that 1-800-GET-HELP is not an actual abuse crisis hot line, and let you know how you can find the help you, or someone you know, might be looking for. If you need a crisis hot line, please find one for your area, even if it takes some looking, Or you may call Childhelp USA National Child Abuse Hotline:

1-800-4-A-CHILD (1-800-422-4453).

It also seemed to me that if I were going to write a story like this, I had a responsibility to say a few things directly to you, the reader. I realize that this is not an easy story to read (or to write).

If abuse has not been a part of your experience, this may have seemed unreal to you. The story is fiction, yet like many stories, it is based strongly on reality. Abuse undoubtedly has affected someone you know. I believe that your understanding more about abuse can make you and others safer.

If you have been abused, I am so very sorry for the pain and confusion and hurt that you have experienced. If the abuse hasn't stopped, it must. You have a right to live free from further abuse. There are many people who will help you.

It takes courage to ask for help, to reveal abuse in order that it stop. It can be hard to talk about, especially when the offender is someone you trusted.

If you think the offender could hurt someone else, you may find it easier to reveal your own abuse. An offender often abuses more than one person, and your speaking up could "start the stopping." Stopping abuse—for you and for others—is the right thing.

Don't buy in to keeping secrets. Secrecy is the offender's weapon to hide the wrongdoing, and it often traps you, and your ability to be at your best. The offender may try to force you into silence by saying it will be your fault if hard things happen when you tell. Don't take on blame for telling about the abuse. The truth is, difficulties may come, but they won't be impossible, and they are the result of what the offender did, not you. Abuse is not your fault.

If you are dealing with abuse of the past, like Trish you may find many issues re-surfacing over and over again. Abuse of the past can be confusing. It's never too late to ask for the help you need, even if you thought it was all behind you.

Healing from abuse can begin now. Ask for help. Though it will be a part of your past, you can move into a wonderful and healthy future.

If you are being drawn to abuse: For readers like Abe who have felt drawn toward incest or sexual abuse, and are able to reach out and ask for help before the crash, the timing is excellent. It may be embarrassing or very hard to do, but please get help immediately. You may feel that you've already gone too far, that there's way too much you're ashamed of. But no matter how bad it seems to you, if you have been able to stop before you've crossed the line, be thankful. It's time to go to work. You will need help, but that help is available. Ask for it. Find it. Prevent the pain and hurt of abuse from becoming a reality.

If you have already crossed the line and want to take responsibility: Like you, I wish so much that it had never happened. The hurt you have caused others is now a part of your life and theirs forever. That is sad. It can't be undone. But if you are at the place where you want to take responsibility to stop any further abuse and do what you can to make amends, you can find a way. It will be hard. But the rest of your life will be better for having begun it now, and the victims of your abuse can also be helped.

I encourage you to gather around you all the support and caring you can find so that you will have others to walk with you, even if they are angry and hurt when they learn what has happened. You will need them.

If you are caught, you will be dealt with by society's justice system. If you ask for help, it may quite likely lead to the same system, but the circumstances could be rather different. Your request for help will indicate an acceptance of accountability. You will have others around you, ready to offer support. Your honesty and openness will allow those working with you to do so most effectively.

What happens will depend on the circumstances of abuse, who is working with you, and the laws and procedures in effect where you live. It would be good to have someone find out what could likely happen, so that you won't feel so afraid when the time comes.

You may say, "I'll just stop, and I'll do it on my own." There are difficulties with that. The greatest one is that you may not be able to stop the abuse without help. You may continue to hurt others, even though you have told yourself you don't want that to happen.

The important thing now is that your abusive acts stop and that you get the help you need. Breaking the secrecy is a big step in breaking the cycle of abuse. Finding someone to talk to is a beginning place.

To those who thought this book was about physics, thanks for joining Abe and Eis, Trish, and Maggie, and me. I hope the story was an adventure into life you're glad you took.